Arguably the most
made, *What's Going On* established Motown
star Marvin Gaye as a unique and maverick
musical talent and simultaneously helped to
re-define the Motown sound. Gaye's
determination and vision resulted not only
in inspirational, pioneering grooves but, in
the era of Vietnam and Civil Rights protests,
an album that challenged America to take a
long, hard look at itself.

By focusing on the story behind the
recording of this seminal work, Ben Edmonds
has produced a riveting and truly original
take on Marvin Gaye. He examines in detail
the making of this masterpiece – initially
rejected by Motown's quality control
department – interviewing many of the
artists and record company employees closest
to the singer, to arrive at a deeper
understanding of what the album means and
of Gaye himself. It is a brilliant yet tragic story.

WHAT'S GOING ON?

What's Going On?

*Marvin Gaye And The
Last Days Of The Motown Sound*

BEN EDMONDS

1

First published in the UK and simultaneously in North America
in 2001 by MOJO Books, an imprint of Canongate Books,
14 High Street, Edinburgh EH1 1TE

10 9 8 7 6 5 4 3 2 1

British Library Cataloguing-in-Publication Data
A catalogue record for this book is available on request
from the British Library

ISBN 1 84195 083 1

Typeset by Patty Rennie Production, Glenbervie
Printed and bound by Grafos, Spain

www.canongate.net

*To my parents, who gave me life;
and to the people of my adopted home Detroit,
who show me every day what it's worth.*

Contents

Acknowledgements

FIRST AND FOREMOST, THANKS MUST BE GIVEN
and praise offered to the many voices who consented to be
represented in these pages. It may have started with my curios-
ity, but it became their story and I thank them for sharing it with
me. I am especially grateful to those who suffered multiple
interview intrusions with grace, and for the friendships I've
made along the way that have already extended beyond the
bounds of this project.

Interview subjects included Elgie Stover, David Van De
Pitte, Frankie Gay, Obie Benson, Joe Schaffner, Steve Smith,
Martha Reeves, Barrett Strong, Hank Cosby, Brenda Holloway,
Jack Ashford, George Clinton, Harry Balk, Paul Riser, the late
Thomas "Beans" Bowles, Johnny Griffith, Kenneth Stover, Walter
Gaines, Fred Gorman, Hank Dixon, Carathman P. Spencer, Ed
Wolfrum, Elaine Jesmer, Johnny Bristol, Ken Sands, Ivy Jo
Hunter, Richard "Pistol" Allen, Russ Terrana, Louvain Demps,
Barney Ales, Uriel Jones, James Green, William "Mickey" Steven-

son, Bob Ohlsson, Lawrence Miles, Ann (Mrs James) Jamerson, Dr Robert Sims, Deke Richards, Bob Babbitt, Sylvia Moy, Calvin Harris, Eddie Willis, Marlene Barrow (Judith Marlene Tate), Janie Bradford, Dave Marsh, Andrew Loog Oldham, Jim Hendin, Joe Messina, Ralph Terrana, George Benson, Jack Brokensha, Bobby Rodgers, Curtis McNair, J.J. Barnes, Art Stewart, Larry Nozero, John Trudell, Dennis Coffey, Dave Dixon, Dan Carlisle, Maxine Powell, Artie Fields, Clay McMurray, Joe Hunter, Frances Nero, André Williams, Felix Resnick, Georgia Ward, Marshall Crenshaw, The Electrifying Mojo, Don Davis, Dayna Hartwick and, in just under the wire, Richard Morris.

I know of no words that will adequately express what the support of my parents Janet and Benjamin L. Edmonds Sr and sisters Nancy Paull and Katharine Paty has meant to me. I am blessed to have such a family.

The encouragement and patience of the MOJO editorial team was equally indispensable: Paul Trynka, who commissioned and edited the original piece; Jim Irvin, who got the snowball rolling on this MOJO book; and Pat Gilbert, upon whose shoulders fell the unenviable task of prying the manuscript away from me.

Special thanks for tea, sympathy and other life support systems: Harry Weinger at Universal Music (above, beyond and then some), Terry Lawson, Steve Byrne and Dale Parry at the Detroit Free Press, Jaan Uhelszki, Maribel Restrepo, Allan "Dr Licks" Slutsky, Susan Whitall and Al Fisk at the Detroit News, Stewart Francke, Rona Chapman, Jimmy Webb, Dr Scott Halzman, Andrew Oldham, Rose and Jerry Lubin, Becky Tyner, Dave Marsh, David Sanjek, Eddie Harsch, Randy Haecker at Sony/Legacy, Dr Steven Feldman, Ann Delisi, Ben Fong-Torres,

Andrew Male, Marie Leighton, the late William Baran, Don Waller, David Fricke, Diane Martin, Geoff Brown, Dan Carlisle, Michael Ochs, Susan Paradise, W. Kim Heron, Felicia Hunt-Taylor at the Charles C. Wright Museum of African-American History (Detroit), Freddie Patterson, Zachary Slovinsky, Wah Wah Watson, Liz Copeland, Larry Beckett, John Carter, Steve Hendin, Elaine Jesmer, David Moss, Jack Ryan, Patti Mitsui, Martin Bandyke, Rosie and Tom Hunter, Judy Henske, Craig Doerge, the still obscene Steven Clean, Marshall Crenshaw, Jenny Bulley, Buzzy Linhart, Matt Lee, Gary Stewart, Weldon McDougall III, F. Rigby Barnes, Harvey Kubernik, Jane and Walter Bernd, Peter and Charles Ransom, Christopher Alex, Amy Herot, Susie Hudson, Bill Levenson, Bruce Cohen, Dana Smart, Paul Barker at the Motown Museum, Ellen Simmons and the staff of the Music and Performing Arts Department at the Detroit Public Library, Gayle Harte, Arthur Allen Paty, Sally Kellog. Anne Williamson, Richard Dewhurst, Maxine and Charles Dewhurst, Jonathan Paull Sr, Jonathan Paull Jr, Alexandra Paull and Benjamin Paull.

In memory of Dave Dixon and Jack Nitzsche, two grumpy old men I miss every day.

The title of Chapter One, "His Own Dark City," comes from an unpublished musical of the same name by Jimmy Webb. The title of Chapter Nine, "Here In The Going, Going, Gone," is a song by Greg Brown. Both were appropriated with the blessing of their authors.

Unless otherwise specified, all chart positions cited are American and come from Billboard magazine, used courtesy of BPI communications and Joel Whitburn Record Research Inc.

Introduction

THIS BOOK IS NOT INTENDED TO BE A BIOG-
raphy of Marvin Gaye, nor is it a history of Motown
Records. You already have multiple choices of both, the
most useful of which you will find listed in our bibli-
ography at the back. This volume is concerned only with
a slice of the Gaye story, but its subject – on the surface a
simple vinyl disc not unlike millions of others – has held
me spellbound for nearly 30 years to the day I am writing
this.

For me, it was love at first listen with the Marvin
Gaye album *What's Going On.* It was June of 1971, and I was
a rock'n'roll kid fortunate to have come of age at a time
when that musical genre meant Otis Redding as much as
The Rolling Stones, Howlin' Wolf as well as the Beach

Boys, Tim Buckley *and* Sly And The Family Stone *and* the MC5. If you happened to be in the hands of an enlightened underground radio guide on the FM side of the dial – as I was also fortunate to be, first from WBCN in Boston and then from WABX in Detroit – you might even be led from the Byrds to the Velvet Underground to John Coltrane in a single set. We were raised to see rock-'n'roll as an emotional ideal as much as a sound, whose truth could be recognised in virtually any form of music. It was about creativity, fearlessness, vision, righteousness, and a ringing "fuck you" in the face of musical convention. Buck Owens was rock'n'roll, but so were Miles Davis, Harry Partch, Charlie Parker, Woody Guthrie and Charles Ives.

Even with such an eclectic grounding, *What's Going On* sounded like nothing I had heard before. Though it has inspired multiple tribute albums and its individual songs have been covered with regularity over the years, nothing in the annals of pop music since – including the illustrious catalog of Mr Gaye himself – has sounded quite like it. "Beyond category", as Duke Ellington was so fond of saying. My instant infatuation with this music has turned into a lifelong love affair. At 35:33 it's not a terribly long album, but damn if it ain't deep. It's been 30 years and, after thousands of dives into its shimmering waves of sound, I haven't gotten anywhere near the bottom of it yet.

As the many works devoted to Marvin and Motown began appearing, none told me all I wanted to know about how this remarkable album came to be. Eventually I was given the opportunity to take a crack at researching and telling the tale myself.

My mission was to unearth fresh testimony and perspectives, so I have quoted from other sources only when their subjects were unavailable to me. I've quoted Marvin sparingly for the same reason; for more from the man himself consult the two full biographies: the trailblazing Divided Soul by David Ritz, and Steve Turner's supplementally valuable Trouble Man. Because Hitsville was a house of many mansions, it was my intention to let other folks have the floor, some for the first time. Marvin broke Motown *omerta* with *What's Going On* by naming the people who did the real work. In that spirit I've tried to give them voices as well. While "the whole story" is something any biographer knows to be an illusion, I hope the time you spend with these people adds to your understanding and appreciation of this miraculous music. Should you object to any of the conclusions I've drawn from what I found, or any of the opinions I've interjected, buy me a drink and we'll talk about it.

This is not simply about a singer and a record album. It is the story of an idea, formed out of the mixed ethers of social anger and spiritual longing, that Marvin Gaye articulated with a cast of brilliant accomplices, and fought to get recorded and released. From that idea, and with that help, and out of that struggle, something was fashioned that continues to touch souls more profoundly than even its creator could have imagined.

In tracing these developments another story presented itself, one I hadn't anticipated when I undertook the journey. There are both advantages and disadvantages to focusing on only a small slice of this artist's life. On the plus side, I get to detail the most glorious moment in Marvin Gaye's career, ignoring for the most part the slow slide toward an inescapable tragedy that his life became after this point. On the minus side, this book does not take place in the golden years of Motown's emergence as the undisputed Sound Of Young America. The Hitsville kingdom I found myself chronicling was, for all its success in this period and beyond, beginning to crumble, as every earthly kingdom must.

What's Going On turned out to be not just Motown's first genuine '60s-style album, but also the last great album made in Detroit before Motown Records did the unthinkable and left its hometown, succumbing to the technicolor siren song of Los Angeles. As I talked with people – some who made the move west, and others who were not invited to – a picture began to emerge of the Motor City abandoned, and of what was left behind. Though I moved to Michigan to become an editor of Creem magazine as the Motown evacuation was beginning, because I had not been a Detroiter as the empire was being built I could not fully comprehend the impact of this abandonment on the soul of the city. Due to length restrictions it must remain a subplot of our story here, but it is a subject that could easily carry a book of its own.

Because this is an American story, unless otherwise indicated all chart positions cited are from the US trade publication Billboard.

Prologue: At The Corner Of Michigan And Trumble

*God loves me and I love God. I try to do His work
as I feel I am supposed to and I do it to the best of
my ability. As a result He blesses me.*

Marvin Gaye

JUNE 28, 1990. IN THE CRUEL LIGHT OF DAY,
Tiger Stadium looks as beat up and run down as the dilap-
idated Detroit neighborhood it sits in. One of the oldest
and once one of the grandest baseball parks in America, a
recently applied coat of paint cannot disguise the past
tense of its glory. But tonight, with an overflow crowd that
exceeds the official estimate of 50,000 by plenty, there is
an electric buzz of anticipation in the air that threatens to
levitate the old ballpark at the corner of Michigan Avenue

and Trumble Street. Aretha Franklin, Stevie Wonder and Frankie Beverly will perform, but this is not a concert, and these great stars are no more than supporting players in this night's drama.

A sleek town car glides across the field to the stage, and the throng erupts at the sight of its passenger, a slim, dignified black man with graying hair. When Nelson Mandela approaches the microphone the rowdy crowd falls silent. The South African freedom fighter is touring America to celebrate his freedom after more than a quarter-century of unjust imprisonment, and few stops on his itinerary are as important as Detroit. In the city that serves, for better and worse – and here there is plenty of both – as the symbol of African-American urban empowerment, Mandela's words carry the weight of the world. "When we were in prison," he tells the adoring throng, "we appreciated and avidly listened to the sound of Detroit, Motortown. On reaching Detroit, I recalled some of the words of the song sung by Marvin Gaye.

> *"Brother, brother," he quotes, "there's far too many of you dying. Mother, mother, there's far too many of you crying . . ."*

At this moment, maybe the stadium *is* levitating. The

crowd knows every inflection of each of these words by heart. They were written here in Detroit, sung and recorded here, and though they now belong to the world, the words of this hit song retain a special resonance in the city of their birth. But Nelson Mandela does not recite them to curry favor with a local audience. Though Marvin Gaye's 1971 album *What's Going On* is now regarded as a landmark musical recording, Mandela's quote from the title song is pointing out that, two decades on, the paint is still fresh on Gaye's portrait of a troubled, turbulent social landscape. The problems Marvin Gaye saw coming to the Detroit of the late 1960s now belong to the world. And Gaye's prescription for these ills – a soulful mixture of compassion, communication, understanding, spiritual awareness and love – still waits to be filled.

We're another decade and a new millennium on from Mandela's reminder, and the relevance of *What's Going On* continues to grow apace with its musical stature. This extraordinary album is the product of Marvin Gaye's spiritual bankruptcy and his personal redemption through music. It is also the product of the deepening twilight of Motown Records' first decade in Detroit, a time and a place and a musical empire the like of which the world will never see again.

1 His Own Dark City

> *The business is tremendously competitive, espe-*
> *cially on the chitlin circuit, because blacks were not*
> *permitted to evolve to popdom. So as a chitlin*
> *circuit artist it's most essential that you churn out*
> *hit after hit or you don't work. You're only as good*
> *as your last record. There is very little chance of*
> *acquiring any major securities as a performer.*
>
> Marvin Gaye

IN 1968 NELSON MANDELA WAS CONFINED TO a tiny cell on Robben Island, a hellish penal colony off the coast of South Africa. Continents away, Marvin Gaye was free to walk the streets of Detroit – heck, the successful soul singer had the choice of walking or being chauffeured – yet he felt no less imprisoned. The walls of his personal prison had closed in dramatically on the night of October 14, 1967 when singing partner Tammi Terrell collapsed into his arms on-stage in Virginia during a performance of Ain't No Mountain High Enough, blacking out from the pain of an undiagnosed brain tumor that would eventually drain her young life completely. His duet records with Terrell had established Gaye as the dreamy male half of America's most romantic musical couple, and combined with his string of solo hits to make him "The Prince of Motown".

This was no paper crown. Since Berry Gordy Jr started the Motown Recording Corporation in 1959 with eight hundred dollars borrowed from a family fund, the upstart little company at 2648 West Grand Boulevard had mushroomed into a multimillion-dollar business. (Or so we must assume. Since Gordy steadfastly refused to open his books to the RIAA for certification, there's no way we'll ever know for sure how many copies any pre-1980 Motown record sold).

The mid-'60s American record industry was frantic to find a Stateside "answer" to The Beatles and the British Invasion bands, banking on everything from folk-rock to psychedelia. In point of fact the answer existed before the English ever issued the challenge. The stable of artists gathered under Gordy's "Sound of Young America" banner – of which Gaye, Smokey Robinson And The Miracles, Mary Wells, the Four Tops, the Temptations, Martha And The Vandellas, the Marvelettes, the Supremes, and Little Stevie Wonder were only the first wave – constituted a one-label counter-invasion force. It looked absurdly presumptuous when Berry Gordy first installed a large sign on the front of the small house on West Grand Boulevard that proclaimed it "Hitsville US". Within a couple of years it was a simple statement of fact.

To the people who labored behind the Hitsville banner, Motown was something much more than America's most successful independent record company, or, as it would soon become, the biggest black-owned business in the entire land of opportunity. "There was a family atmosphere from day one," says Martha Reeves, who came in as a secretary and left as a star. "When I first arrived there, Pops Gordy [Berry Gordy Sr] nearly whacked me with a two-by-four he was carrying through a doorway. He was remodeling the space that the former owner had used as his photographic studio, turning it into a recording studio. He did it plank by plank. Berry was running around with his sleeves rolled up; he seemed to be everywhere at once. Mother Gordy was there offering encouragement, and the place was full of friends and family pitching in. Everyone who worked for Motown in the early days felt like they'd helped build the place. It was a family relationship."

The company sprang from humble origins. "When I came there it wasn't even Motown yet, it was the Rayber Music Company," recalls Richard Morris. "They used to advertise on the radio: 'If you're a songwriter and want your material recorded, call Trinity 6–7285.' I made an appointment, and it was my good fortune to be auditioned by Smokey Robinson, who was getting quite a reputation as a songwriter. Afterward I was talking with Raynoma Liles Gordy. She was Berry's wife, the Ray of Rayber and a real motivating force in the early days of the company. We'd gone to high school together, and she asked if I'd like to stick around and do a few things.

"When I leaped at the chance she said, 'You can start by mopping the floor,' and then she had me wash the walls and windows. I didn't care because I was close to music; I even asked to come back the next day. That was the day they installed the recording equipment Berry had bought from DJ Bristoe Bryant. With Robert Bateman and Brian Holland, I began to study the recording set-up. After a few days of making myself useful, they offered me a full-time job. My starting salary was $5 a week." Morris would grow into a hit-making producer, and the little

Rayber family operation on West Grand Boulevard would become a multi-million dollar international business called Motown.

This is very much a saga of the American Midwest, which means it is a story of hard work. In the deceptively stable bliss of post-World War II America, the midwestern heartland was a place where people labored, bought homes, raised families, and had the expectation that their simple adherence to the ivy-covered verities of Benjamin Franklin, Thomas Jefferson and Dwight David "Ike" Eisenhower would keep the skies cloudless and the future infinitely agreeable.

Chicago was the great brute of the Midwest, a place where they chewed stuff up and spat it out as something else. With its endless stockyards and stench of animal slaughter, it was a natural home to the blues. Slightly to the East was its twin Midwestern tower Detroit, a city that lived in the shadow of Chicago's hulking mass, but had a personality all its own. It was no less industrial than its bigger brother, but was a city of ideas, a place where things were conceived and then made. Instead of cold steel and rotting meat, Motortown turned out gleaming, fantastic dream machines. Henry Ford's two great ideas were the automobile, and the assembly line manufacturing system that would make his creation available to almost everyone. Ford gave the world a picture of Detroit as a benevolent assembly line. What Berry Gordy Jr added to this picture was a soundtrack.

Gordy didn't invent the crossover of rhythm and blues into the musical mainstream, but he damn well perfected it. Black enterprises like Vivian Carter and Jimmy Bracken's Vee-Jay Records in Chicago and Don Robey's Duke-Peacock operation in Houston, as well as white-owned labels like Atlantic and Starday-King, that had sprung up in the more segregated '50s to cater to the niche markets of R&B, blues and jazz, had all experienced a swell of their base audience by the interest of the young, white rock'n'roll mainstream. This had been Berry Gordy's *raison-d'être* from day one. As a child of the assembly line, he had seen people of all colors, creeds and nationalities working shoulder-to-shoulder, so he was perfectly positioned to receive the vision of these people standing in a rainbow queue to purchase his product, which would be crafted on an assembly line of its own.

"My own dream for a hit factory was quickly taking form," Gordy wrote in his autobiography To Be Loved, "a concept that had been shaped by principles I had learned on the Lincoln-Mercury assembly line. At the plant the cars started out as just a frame, pulled along on conveyor belts until they emerged at the end of the line – brand spanking new cars rolling off the line. I wanted the same concept for my company, only with artists and songs and records. I wanted a place where a kid could walk in one door an unknown and come out another a recording artist – a star."

(This workplace integration, which had been accomplished with as much blood as sweat and tears, did not mean either racial equality or harmony, and did not spill over into the streets or schools to any appreciable degree, as most any African-American resident of Detroit would have told you. The picture Henry Ford painted looked like salvation from a seat of poverty in the rural South, but up close there was all manner of racial fine print that couldn't be read from such distances. So even as hopeful black workers had streamed into the Motor City decades earlier, there was already an underpinning of disappointment that would in time turn into anger and finally revolt. For the time being, however, the economy was good and jobs were plentiful, leading to the growth of a black middle class that actively encouraged young men like Berry Gordy Jr to dream impossible dreams, and in so doing accomplish more than anyone else would have thought possible. And if working in close proximity didn't lead to racial and ethnic harmony, it certainly fostered a shared desire to escape the numbing, soul-draining drudgery of the assembly line. This was something Gordy could work with whatever the racial or political disposition. His songs gave workers something to whistle on the line, and something to relax and party with after the workday was done.)

Being Motown's leading man, their number one male solo singer, meant that Marvin Gaye had a seat of distinction at the family table. Gaye had arrived in Detroit in 1960 as the protégé of Moonglows mastermind Harvey Fuqua, having apprenticed in the final lineup of that revered doo-wop group. Fuqua quickly hooked up with Gwen Gordy, and the joining of their business interests – her Anna Records became their Harvey and Tri-Phi labels – was consecrated when the two became man and wife. When Gwen's ambitious brother Berry absorbed both labels, Marvin found himself the property of Motown Records and assigned to its Tamla subsidiary. He worked his way in as a session drummer and pianist, but it was always understood that this shy, soft-spoken young man was destined for greater things.

"When I was just an A&R secretary," recalls Martha Reeves, "I knew him as a session musician first. When he would come to the studio, he'd wear glasses and keep a pipe in his mouth, wearing a Sinatra-style hat that was always pulled down over his eyes. So nobody got a good look at him unless he wanted them to. And he always arrived on his own timetable. He was always late, but he was so dependably late that I learned to inform him that the date would start a couple of hours before it really did, and then he'd show up on time. I never minded going out of my way for Marvin, because there was something about him that told you you were dealing with a special person." This air of singularity was elevated considerably when he began dating and then married Anna Gordy, another of Berry's sisters.

What none of these outside observers, including Anna Gaye, could have known was that beneath his gentle, bashful exterior lay an angry, bottomless sea of secret torments, barely submerged self-loathing and shame. By his good manners and impressive command of the Bible, most judged him the product of a proper upbringing. Yet Marvin almost never mentioned his family back in DC, and with good reason. It was true that his father, the Reverend Marvin Gay Sr, was an Elder of a "Hebrew Pentecostal" church called the House of God – its full designation was the House of God, the Holy Church of the Living God, the Pillar and Ground of the

Truth, the House of Prayer for All People – and had imprinted the sect's strict and near-Judaic interpretation of Biblical truth on all his four children. But beyond this steel curtain of righteousness lived a cross-dressing, womanising, cruelly mercurial man who thought nothing of berating and beating the woman whose weekly pay-check was all that kept the family from the street. The rod was not spared when it came to the children either. Eldest child Marvin Jr would get the worst of it, stepping in as he invariably did to deflect his father's vicious attention away from his younger siblings or his mother. No, his father's house was not a subject he cared to talk about. It had been something to be endured and escaped at the first opportunity. He'd made his getaway, but wasn't he also abandoning his post as protector of those younger and weaker than himself? He was already running confused.

He wasn't simply running away from home, he was running toward music, yet even his greatest gift was a source of confusion. Doo wop had been his ticket out of town, and though this romantic vocal harmony music hardly presented the overt threat of hip-swiveling rockabilly or the frenzied outer edge of R&B, Marvin understood that he had crossed a line that separated him from the church music through which his gift had been revealed. Was he not only running away from his father, but from his father's God?

The conflicted young man was definitely in the market for a father figure, and Marvin Gaye was fortunate enough to find two of the best in the music business, benefiting from the old-school knowledge of Harvey Fuqua and the determined widescreen dreaming of Berry Gordy. Yet even this good fortune turned out to be tainted, at least in the mind of Marvin Gaye. All was fine when he arrived in Detroit as Fuqua's chosen protégé, and felt he was being groomed for greatness on one of his mentor's new record labels. When Gwen Gordy and Harvey folded their business into Berry Gordy's, the singer found himself part of a deal that delivered him to another father figure without his knowledge or consent. To be treated like a commodity came as a shock to the sensitive young singer. When he discovered that the wily Fuqua had sold only 50 per cent of his stake in the singer to Gordy, his shock took on a darker hue. To Marvin, it seemed like his "fathers" had already carved him up like a side of beef. On the surface all was hunky-dory, but there was a disillusionment that was already seething before his career even got into gear. Marvin was one of Motown's first starry-eyed singers to learn the difference between business and family.

After a couple of false starts as a pop crooner, Marvin had his breakthrough hit when Mickey Stevenson produced Stubborn Kind Of Fellow in 1962. (When background singers were needed for the session, it also caused Martha Reeves to pull together the group that would become her Vandellas.) It was ironic that Motown, a label frequently accused of smoothing out the hard-core edge of R&B, should take their artist with the smoothest delivery and package him as a rock'n'roll belter. But your first hit for Motown almost always constructed the box you'd occupy as an artist, and Stubborn Kind Of Fellow, followed by the equally aggressive Hitch Hike, typecast Marvin Gaye as a rock'n'roll singer. After Frank Sinatra and Nat King Cole, he named his four major vocal influences as Clyde McPhatter, Rudy West of the Five Keys, Little Willie John and Ray Charles. (We must also mention Jimmy Scott, the inspiration for the ballad album eventually called *Vulnerable*, which Marvin obsessed over a decade and would not be released for two decades after that.) Brother Ray's secular shouting was the only part of his hero's arsenal Gaye was vocally unsuited to emulate, but this was right where his first couple of hits positioned him.

"You know how hard he pushed on Hitch Hike?" asks recording engineer James Green. "I'd hear that and say, 'Marvin, if you keep doing that you're gonna lose your cords, man.' For someone with his quality of voice, you don't want to hear him straining like that. But that's what Berry Gordy wanted. He had everyone in a niche, and he was very upfront about telling you what he wanted. He wanted this one doing that, and that one doing this. He's a businessman and the president of the company, and he wants things the way he wants them. But as I came to understand, he had those niches for everybody because he was the only one who was seeing the whole of the company, and trying to keep a balance to everything he had going."

Once his particular niche was established, Gaye recorded with the many producers crucial to Gordy's mushrooming empire. Principal among them were the Holland-Dozier-Holland team (Can I Get A Witness, You're A Wonderful One, How Sweet It Is (To Be Loved By You)) and Smokey Robinson (I'll Be Doggone, Ain't That Peculiar). As uncomfortable as he sometimes felt in his rock'n'roll skin – especially when he was asked to be the aggressive live performer the early records demanded – the singles were hits and often great records. Hitch Hike also became a staple of rock bands in garages everywhere, thanks to an underwhelming cover by The Rolling Stones and the theft of its distinctive riff by the Velvet Underground in There She Goes Again.

The romantic side that he'd sought to showcase as a crooner was utilised by Motown in a series of successful duets with several of the label's ladies: first Mary Wells (What's The Matter With You Baby), then Kim Weston (It Takes Two), and finally and most spectacularly with Tammi Terrell (Your Precious Love, Ain't No Mountain High Enough, Ain't Nothing Like The Real Thing, You're All I Need To Get By). With both sides of his rock 'n' romance persona nailed down, Marvin Gaye looked to the world like one happy kinda fella.

In reality the Prince Of Motown was at the bottom end of a vicious cycle of depression, for which his professional accomplishments offered not the slightest compensation. They were in fact a large part of the problem. His hit records – glittering pop-rock vehicles manufactured on Berry Gordy's Motown assembly line, in which his voice was frequently treated like nothing more than another component – mocked him. Measured against the lifelong inspiration of the artistry of Sinatra and Nat Cole, Marvin Gaye judged himself to be a gold-plated fraud.

Some of the duets with Tammi Terrell were literally fraudulent. Following her collapse, Terrell's crippling headaches began returning with alarming regularity. Determined to seize the golden professional moment, she gamely tried to keep up with the duo's touring and recording schedule. But she started missing shows, and eventually performing live became too taxing altogether. She hung on in the studio a bit longer – some reports had her singing her last parts from a wheelchair – but it was a losing battle. When the source of her condition was finally diagnosed and its gravity exposed, she was sent home to Philadelphia for good. She underwent a series of unsuccessful brain surgeries that progressively sapped her strength. Tammi Terrell would never sing another note.

But America couldn't get enough of its singing sweethearts, and the Motown machine needed to be fed, so Valerie Simpson (who co-wrote and produced many of the duets with husband Nick Ashford) was drafted to impersonate Terrell in the studio. A reluctant Marvin was pressured into participating by the company's "suggestion" that the hits needed to keep on coming to cover Tammi's medical bills. He complied, but it must have been like a dagger in his heart every time he heard these fake duets on the radio. One of them, The Onion Song, became an unexpected hit in the UK. (It was the only Marvin and Tammi record to crack the UK top ten, something this scribe from the Colonies is at a loss to explain.) Normally this would have thrilled the Anglophile singer.

Now the news only pushed Marvin further into the depression that was never far away even under the most favorable conditions.

His personal life was in utter disarray. His marriage to the boss's sister Anna Gordy was marked by violent clashes and accusatory silences. He was being hounded by the government for back taxes. He was estranged from his own family and ambivalent about the Motown family into which he'd been sold. He felt, by turns, overwhelmed with despair and utterly hollow. He contemplated suicide, and once barricaded himself in an apartment with a gun and had to be talked down by his beloved father-in-law Pops Gordy. When he recorded a version of Yesterday, he invested the lyric with a yearning only sketched by Paul McCartney:

> *Yesterday all my troubles seemed so far away*
> *now I need a place to hide away . . .*
> *Suddenly, people, I ain't half the man I used to be*
> *there's a heavy* heavy *shadow hanging over me . . .*

2 The Prince Of Motown Plots

I don't like to follow my footsteps and my shadow.
Singers are afraid to branch out and try something
new and exciting. But I wasn't.

Marvin Gaye

THE SHADOW OVER MARVIN GAYE DID NOT
lift when, quite by accident, he found himself with the
biggest-selling single in Motown history. Norman
Whitfield had cut I Heard It Through The Grapevine
with Marvin in 1967, but Quality Control – the department that picked and scheduled the releases at the
company's weekly product evaluation meetings – passed
over the brooding, ominous-sounding track in favor of
the comparatively undistinguished Holland-Dozier-

Holland production Your Unchanging Love. Berry Gordy's reasoning seemed to be that this song better conformed to the singer's established romantic image.

Engineer Bob Ohlsson cut the reference discs played at these meetings, and often got to play fly on the wall. "They had a litmus test at one point," he says. "They'd play the top five singles on the chart at that moment, and anything considered for release had to sequence somewhere among those hits. It had to fit. That was the hold-up on Grapevine. Norman got quite heated, but let's face it – the record sounded like nothing else out there, let alone in the top five. That doomed it by the standards they were using then."

Norman Whitfield was flabbergasted. He had recognised Grapevine as his potential *pièce de résistance* when Barrett Strong first played him the rudiments of the song in the summer of 1966. Strong had sung Motown's very first hit, Money, and was among the first to leave the company. Working in Chicago for Vee-Jay Records, he heard the Temptations on the radio and figured that Motown might be ready for the more soulful sounds he was most at home with. Back in Detroit with a $40 piano on which only 10 keys worked, he hammered out the frameworks for two songs he was sure would put him back on the map at Motown. One was a ballad with a lovely piano figure that would become I Wish It Would Rain. For the other he had a bluesy feel based loosely on his main man Ray Charles, a bass line and the phrase "I heard it through the grapevine." When Whitfield heard those six words, says Barrett, "he was off to the races." Thus was born the songwriting team whose funkier, more street-level orientation would be the primary color of Motown's second golden era.

In Grapevine Norman Whitfield had a horse he could ride all the way into immortality as a producer. When he first cut it in August 1966 it was earmarked for the Isley Brothers, possibly intended as a followup to their Motown bow This Old Heart Of Mine, but wound up being sung by Smokey Robinson And The Miracles. (Whether the Isleys ever got a crack at the song is the subject of some debate. Ronald Isley has always said they did, citing this as a prime example of Motown's alleged practice of taking choice material away from them. To date no corroborating tape evidence has been located in the company vaults.) The Miracles' version is breezily paced, like Smokey already knows the answer to the questions he's asking his unfaithful lover and, contrary to what the words say, wants to move on as much as she does.

When Whitfield recorded the song again the following February – assigned this time to the

Temptations initially, though the track would become Marvin's – he kept the arrangement very similar to the original, but cut the tempo in half. This may be the masterstroke of Norman Whitfield's entire career. Slowed down, the rattlesnake rhythm and Paul Riser's accusatory strings unlocked all the song's poisons – the anxiety, the desperation, the paranoia – and made it the perfect musical bed on which to lay what many regard as the most impassioned vocal performance Marvin Gaye ever gave. Whitfield pushed and pushed and then pushed some more to get it; the producer and singer reportedly almost came to blows during the vocal session. It was set in a key beyond the singer's natural reach, so that he'd have no choice but to strain for it, a trick the producer employed regularly throughout his career. "That used to *really* make me mad," relates Dennis Edwards of The Tempattions, "but then when the record would wind up in the Top 10 I wouldn't be quite so angry." But whatever discomfort Marvin may have felt, the result would have justified twice the torture. Gaye was forced to tap into his personal reservoir of anguish, and all the blood wound up on Whitfield's magnificent track. If the *What's Going On* album would be the ultimate justification for an artist producing himself, then Grapevine is an equally powerful argument for why an artist should not.

Together, Whitfield and Gaye dredged up what Dave Marsh called "a lost continent of music and emotion" when naming Grapevine the best single of all time in his book The Heart Of Rock & Soul. Such accolades would not have surprised the supremely confident Whitfield one bit. He knew exactly what he had, and the company's rejection forced him into another course of action. The supremely annoyed Whitfield recorded an Aretha Franklin-inspired arrangement of Grapevine on Gladys Knight And The Pips and watched it shoot to Number 2 pop and Number 1 R&B in the autumn of '67. The bland Gaye record they'd chosen over his Grapevine had stalled out, a development that pleased Whitfield no end, at least when it wasn't irritating him beyond belief.

Still convinced that Marvin's version could be an even bigger hit, he continued to lobby Berry Gordy for its release. "Norman believed in that record so strongly he almost lost his job over it," chuckles Barrett Strong. "He kept pushing and pushing, until Berry finally said, 'Get out my face. Mention that fucking record again and you're fired!'" To placate the persistent producer it was included as filler on Marvin's August 1968 album *In The Groove*, ironically released the same month as the Smokey Robinson And the Miracles LP *Special Occasion*, which contained the original Grapevine as filler. Marvin's version lit up the phones when a Chicago DJ with adventurous ears broke format and aired it as an album track in October. Within weeks the *In The Groove* album had been facelifted and reissued as *I Heard It Through The Grapevine*, and the rush-released 45 stayed at Number 1 on both the pop and R&B charts for seven weeks. Norman Whitfield's moody thunderbolt had not only obliterated his own million-selling version with Gladys Knight, it had sold more copies than any Motown record before it.

Marvin was not terribly impressed by this explosive turn of events. He'd admitted some jealousy when the Gladys version hit, feeling he'd been denied a winner. Nobody with an ego could fail to derive some pleasure from having a Number 1 record the size of Godzilla, but because of the recording circumstances Marvin would always feel somewhat ambivalent about his biggest hit single. The satisfaction he derived from it lay mostly in seeing Motown proven resoundingly wrong. He'd had a contentious relationship with the label from day one, acquiring a reputation as a difficult recording artist, a diffident live performer and, in a sort of passive-aggressive way that became his trademark as much as any vocal mannerism, a troublemaker. In later years he'd admit to sometimes having worked overtime to earn his rep.

"Marvin could be a headache for a producer, no

doubt about that," testifies Hank Cosby, who acted in that capacity with the singer on a few occasions. "Many times you'd have to drive over to his house, get him out of bed and drag his ass into the studio. He always lived by his own clock, but it was almost like if you were producing Marvin, he wanted you to demonstrate how important the session was to you. Once you did that and got him to the studio, he'd give you everything you wanted and more."

But the too-easygoing singer who needed coaxing into the studio was only one of the many Marvins his friends and associates would come to know. "For such a mild-mannered guy on the outside, he had a lot of pit bull in him when it came to something he was after," says writer/producer Ivy Jo Hunter. "He was quite a nego-tiator. The first time I saw it was when he gave me the title Dancing In The Street. Mickey Stevenson and I suggested what we thought was a fair percentage of the song for contributing those four words, and he didn't agree. *Definitely* did not agree. He wanted more, and he held out until he got it. There was a rigidity in his resolve not to be moved from his position. He was a stubborn kind of fellow – that was more than just a song title."

What the fellow didn't like about having the biggest hit in Motown history was the increased call for those things about stardom he found most distasteful. At the top of this list was selling himself live, a chore he'd never been comfortable with and which he now referred to derisively as "having to go out and stomp the grapes".

"One thing that he was very clear about was that he did not enjoy performing," said his West Coast publicist Elaine Jesmer. "He hated having to go out on that stage. The way he seemed to handle it was to become part of the music. He became an instrument. You could see it – he closed his eyes and never looked at the audience. In those days he never played a show with his eyes open! He didn't consider himself to be graceful, though of course he was in ways he couldn't see. So he stood very still and became a member of the orchestra. That's one of the reasons musicians loved to work with him. Even then, they loved him."

The musos loved him, but show promoters got another Marvin. "We were scheduled to play the Apollo one time, the old four show a day grind," remembered road manager Joe Schaffner, who'd traveled with neighborhood pal Barrett Strong in the earliest days, before Motown even knew what a road manager was. Schaffner toured with many of the label's acts but had a special relationship with the young Prince Of Motown. "Marvin didn't want to do four shows, and told Bobby Schiffman, the son of the original Apollo owner, that we wouldn't do more than two. He was contractually committed to four, but he just refused to do it. When showtime came that day, we were still in Detroit. In fact, we left the house and headed up to Palmer Park so he could play a round of golf. *Then* we got in the car and headed for the airport. He made sure that we arrived in New York in time to do only the final shows, at eight and 10 o'clock. He wasn't going to have it any other way."

"Marvin was Marvin." You'll hear that phrase repeated again and again to explain some exasperating or contradictory bit of behavior. The title of the David Ritz biography Divided Soul couldn't be more apt. Marvin Gaye was a complex and deeply conflicted man – the Pentecostal minister's son who sold sex for a paycheck, the classy crooner who sang meaningless rock'n'roll nursery rhymes, the wise man who often acted like a spoilt child, the natural collaborator whose unnatural ego demanded that he always have the upper hand, the stage-frightened performer who regularly stripped to his skivvies on his final tour in 1983, the lover who thought he was a fighter, the holy artist and the deeply flawed human being. His conflicts, complexes and contradictions ran as deep as his talent.

The contradiction on his plate at this moment was as big

as the sales of Grapevine. His success was impressive to look at, but seemed to him like one of those movie mansion façades constructed for the set of Gone With The Wind with nothing but thin air behind them. He believed his destiny was to be an artist of genuine substance. Perhaps at the instigation of his minister father, Marvin had always felt a divine hand plotting his path. "When I was a child I used to have these dreams," he once told an interviewer. "There were fields of humanity . . . I was singing for what seemed like millions of people." These were apparently more than adolescent fantasies of stardom; as he explained it, he was bathed in a palpable sense of mission. His felt his voice was meant to serve some higher purpose, and though he wasn't yet sure what it might be, he had a sneaking suspicion that it would not involve singing Hitch Hike.

"My first experience with Marvin," recalls Clay McMurray, "was when I was Norman Whitfield's assistant and they were putting the vocals on Grapevine. There were moments when Marvin would have his own feel for things, but because he was the artist and Norman was the producer, he respected the parameters of that professional situation and went wherever Norman directed him. And Norman pushed the hell out of him on Grapevine. That was the way Norman worked with just about every artist, including the Temptations. I could sense that Marvin was not always pleased with the directions he was being taken in. But rather than be confrontational, which was not his style, if things got too uncomfortable he'd call for a break and be out the door."

Marvin had come to the decision that he would no longer be a tool, even as brilliant a tool as he'd been in the hands of Norman Whitfield on I Heard It Through The Grapevine. But he also knew enough about the system he was taking on to understand that until he had a power base he would be nothing *but* a tool. In the Motown system, the power rested with the writer/producers.

"The records were more the expressions of the producers and writers than the artists," states Barrett Strong. "I know that Norman always saw himself as the star of his records; didn't matter *who* was singing on them. You have to have some of that attitude to get your message across to the artist. But the best producers were the ones that matched the right artist to the message in the first place. At that time the producers had ultimate control, at least as far as the making of the records."

This was the sort of control the Prince Of Motown hungered for. So Marvin Gaye – the rebel, the trouble-maker, the outsider – resolved to become a power player within the system.

What a system it was. When Marvin's Grapevine was Number 1 the last week of December '68, Motown had the top three singles, and five of the top ten. (For the record, the others were Number 2: For Once In My Life by Stevie Wonder, Number 3: Love Child by Diana Ross And The Supremes, Number 7: I'm Gonna Make You Love Me by the Supremes and Temptations, and Number 10: Cloud Nine by the Temptations.) Grapevine would stay at Number 1 for seven weeks. Even more astonishingly, no other label could dislodge Motown from the top three positions for a full month.

Though it looked from the outside like an impregnable fortress, within Motown palace intrigues were being played out. The first public expression of what had been percolating behind the scenes had come that October, when the Holland-Dozier-Holland team quit Motown and announced it was suing the company for $22 million over accounting discrepancies and unfulfilled partnership promises. As writer/producers H-D-H had been responsible for the incredible string of Number 1 records by the Supremes that indelibly imprinted Motown as "The Sound Of Young America", and backed it up with hits by the Tops, Tempts, Marvin, Martha and virtually everybody else that the company's revolving system of production made available to them. But Brian

Holland, Lamont Dozier and Eddie Holland came to resent a breakneck work ethic that was rewarded (in their view) with slow and insufficient compensation. To express their displeasure, the trio orchestrated a work slowdown in late 1967. Motown responded by suing them for non-productivity, which was answered with the October '68 walkout. The dispute would keep the team on the sidelines for the next two years, and would not be fully settled for decades, but many people thought that when the three walked out the door they were taking the Motown Sound with them.

Motown's unprecedented chart showing during that Christmas of 1968, which did not include a single Holland-Dozier-Holland production, did much to assuage the fears of those who questioned whether the company had the creative resources to survive H-D-H's departure. But there was no denying the emotional shockwaves that their action generated, and the ripples were felt throughout the company. There was one especially telling organisational change. Because Brian Holland had been in charge of the creative department, that important position would have to be filled. Some had grumbled that Holland's administration cherry-picked the best projects for H-D-H and left the other producers to fight over the table scraps. But they were horrified when the creative department was added to the province of vice-president of corporate affairs Ralph Seltzer, a lawyer whose greatest creativity was exercised in the implementation of fiscal restraint. "Man, don't get me started on *that* gentleman," growls staff arranger Paul Riser, whose musical settings had virtually defined Motown's previous four years of chart domination. "We had requested a piano, and his response was to ask us what we needed with a piano. In the *arranging department*. Can you believe that? But that was the kind of mentality we found ourselves dealing with more and more."

Another mentality was creeping into the creative side as well. The Billboard blitz was an impressive feat, but it was also an indication of the entire industry's all-too-willing descent into blockbuster consciousness. Of course, Motown had never been about anything but having hits, but now there was a bounty on them. "That was when we started getting bonuses for chart position," remembers arranger David Van De Pitte. "If you went Top 20 or Top 10 you got so much, and for a Number 1 you got so much more. It was certainly nice to see the support players get something more for their work, *but* the competition went bananas. That's when the whole nature of the competition changed."

Healthy competition had been the key to

Motown's success. When an artist needed a new record, Berry Gordy threw out the challenge to his many combinations of writer/producers, and whoever came up with the best song got the record. Then he might have two or three different engineers mix the track, each knowing the others were also taking a crack at it. Gordy, who'd performed all these functions himself in the company's earliest days, was liable to jump in at any stage. "Berry and I used to mix together a lot," says engineer Russ Terrana. "We'd challenge each other, and get into some real mixing duels. Producers often requested me for sessions, but Berry wanted me to mix exclusively, because he said that was the crucial point. I loved mixing because I did it by myself; producers were almost never allowed in the mix room. The exception, of course, was Berry. Going back and forth on mixes with him was maybe my favorite experience there. He was a fierce competitor, but he brought out the best in me."

As the company was growing, this competition brought out the best in everybody. Once Motown exploded this changed. Not only was the view from the top different, there was much less room to dance way up there at the tip of the pyramid. If the Holland-Dozier-Holland team was the dominant production personality of the first Motown golden era, then the emergence of an individual, Norman Whitfield, to dominate the second is not without meaning. At Motown, the home of "one for all" assembly line teamwork (complete with a company fight song composed by Smokey Robinson), it was beginning to feel more than a little like every man for himself.

Engineer Ed Wolfrum remembers Marvin at the studios of Motown competitor Golden World Records during the time he first became interested in record production, hanging out at the sessions of his friend J.J. Barnes, an up-and-coming singer with a smooth delivery frequently compared to Marvin's, who recorded for the Golden World-associated labels Ric-Tic and Groovesville. When contacted, however, J.J. Barnes says it must have been somebody else's sessions, because their "relationship" was too strange and strained to qualify as friendship. The story Barnes tells shows that Gaye, in his characteristically passive-aggressive fashion, could be as nastily competitive as any of the big boys in playing the game.

"I was playing the Twenty Grand club," Barnes explains, "and I was somewhat shocked to see him sitting in the audience. See, the night before his wife Anna had come in. I had never met Anna, but when I came out of the dressing room after the show she was waiting for me right by the front of the stage. She introduced herself, and then the woman kissed me! A *real* kiss, in front of everybody at the Twenty Grand. I could never understand what would make her come up and kiss a total stranger like that, but she definitely made sure the entire club witnessed it. I was married myself, and to tell you the truth I found this embarrassing. I don't know what kind of games those two were playing; I guess she was trying to make her man jealous. Next night there he was. Didn't say anything; just sat there and stared. Later, after my contract had been acquired by Motown as part of the Golden World deal, I ran into him one day coming out of the company building on Woodward Avenue. He said, 'Man, you know, you're a *bad* motherfucker.' I didn't really know how to take that, because the term has so many meanings. So I just told him he was too . . .'"

Earlier reports have portrayed Marvin as an active hindrance to Barnes's progress at Motown, a characterisation J.J. confirms. "He was. That's a fact, a definite fact," Barnes says emphatically, but with surprisingly little rancor. "The word was given to me by Eddie Holland, who was then the A&R director. It was straight from Eddie's mouth, and he'd just spoken with Marvin. I guess he'd heard some of the stuff I'd been cutting, and had a fit. 'Hey, this guy is too close to me, bla bla bla. One of us has to go.' Eddie came to me and said, 'Man, Marvin is pitchin' a bitch with Berry and all of us. The conclusion is that we're going to have to change your style.' I asked him what he meant by that. He said, 'Well, unless we come up with something *so different from what you usually do*' – those were his exact words: so different from what you usually do – 'you can't expect to get a record released.' Right then I knew I had to get away from there. What I usually do is be me, and theirs obviously was not a system that was going to work for me."

In the early Motown system, there was even a protocol involving the car you owned. "Much like offices have assigned spaces for you to park," explains keyboard player Johnny Griffith, "you weren't allowed to have certain cars until you reached a certain level. It was like a class system. At first only upper echelon management could buy Cadillacs. Then when the producers started making money they were permitted to buy them too. Finally it filtered down to the musicians. But if a musician bought a Cadillac before it was considered proper, they'd stop calling you on sessions for a while. You didn't know your place, and also if you could afford a Cadillac, what did you need with them? So I enjoyed my Cadillacs out of town. Every weekend I'd fly somewhere to do a session, and I'd have me a Cadillac convertible waiting at the airport. When I came back home, I drove an old Buick."

This was the climate in which Marvin Gaye was attempting to become a player. Though the success of Grapevine would give him a little leverage, as would his marriage to Anna Gordy (depending on where their emotional see-saw stood at any given moment), he was smart enough to know that his plan to become a writer/producer would not be won by petulant outbursts of the sort J.J. Barnes described, but would ultimately turn on his attention to the basics on both sides of the slash.

As a song factory, Motown was like a midwestern Brill Building. Each individual cell buzzed with activity as the teams of writers and producers attempted to go the guys (and maybe gals, though there were noticeably fewer of them) in the next cubicle one better. "Motown had the strongest writers' farm in the universe!" proclaims Elgie Stover, a Jobete writer who'd become Marvin's *aide-de-camp* during the *What's Going On* period. "There were so many writers, and so much great material coming forth, that you could start at one end of the building and by the time you worked your way to the other end you'd have enough new songs to fill an album. Hell, they'd pay you $50 if they were stuck on a word or a line, and more for a title. Ron Miller gave me $200 because a song I was pitching, Once In A Lifetime, caused him to come up with For Once In

My Life, which he took for this other song he'd been working on."

Marvin Gaye's name will be found as a co-composer of several great early Motown records – Beechwood 45789, Hitch Hike, and Dancing In The Street among them – but it was a talent he had never conscientiously applied himself to developing. With Elgie Stover, who'd come to Detroit from Cleveland as a member of a group called the Challengers to record for Harvey Fuqua's Tri-Phi Records and would be among Marvin's most faithful collaborators throughout this period, he set about doing so. Also contributing was Anna Gordy Gaye.

"That was the day of the Motown teams like Holland-Dozier-Holland," says Stover. "Gaye-Stover-Gaye, that was our team. Marvin and I did most of the writing, but Anna found her way in there, in inspiration as well as work. Anna and I stayed up at night working on words, what Marvin used to call 'drunken lyrics,' and then he'd get up and we'd work on music the next day. We turned out three or four songs – or at least three or four 'drunken lyrics' – a night. We wrote a song called Court Of The Common Plea, intended for Ray Charles, and a bunch of songs when Marvin was thinking about doing an album with Sammy Davis Jr. We lost quite a few when little Marvin [son Marvin Pentz Gaye III] was playing with the tape recorder and accidentally erased a whole reel." This was the core team, though Marvin would enlist several other collaborators when he was finally ready to capture the music he kept hearing rush by him like gusts of melodic wind.

The presence of Anna on the creative team was unexpected, given the tempestuous nature of their relationship. "You have to understand me," Marvin explained to biographer David Ritz. "One day I'd be throwing bottles at Anna, and the next day I'd be loving her like we'd just met. Fighting stimulated us. Besides, Anna was always good for my music. She'd give me ideas and push me any way she could. I'm the sort of artist who can always use a push. My moods can get a little heavy."

Anna Gordy Gaye could match her husband mood for mood. Seventeen years his senior (Marvin's second wife would be his junior by the same number of years), Anna may have also had the physical edge over her soft, skinny mate. She was usually judged the winner when their verbal bickering turned into all-out battle. Physical confrontation was nothing new to Marvin, whose contentious nature had earned the child regular beatings from the vengefully inflexible Reverend Gay. Where his father's weapon of choice was a beltstrap (sometimes including the buckle), Anna found that one of her shoes would usually do the trick. An argument at their wedding reception was settled with a shoe-shot to her new husband's head, much to the amusement of his assembled pals.

But there was, as Marvin indicated, just as much love. The union of Harvey Fuqua and Gwen Gordy had been seen in some quarters as more of a merger than a marriage. Marvin, however, was clearly smitten with Anna, according to Elaine Jesmer: "This man was no fool; he was perfectly aware of the political advantages in being married to a Gordy. And Marvin was really good at finding women to take care of him, defenders who'd fight the battles he couldn't or didn't want to. But there was no question, at least when he talked to me, that he loved Anna deeply. He would have been incapable of doing it for politics alone. He needed love above all else. As you've gathered, he was a hugely complicated man." As volatile as their marriage was, Anna always stood by her man creatively. She didn't understand his need to rebel against the company, because this meant rebelling against her brother, but she knew her husband possessed an artistic depth that the company had barely scratched the surface of. She was supportive, and in the battle Marvin was about to fight he was going to need very bit of support he could muster.

His model for the writer/producer/artist he wanted to become was Smokey Robinson. Yet Robinson, whose Miracles were the first act signed to Motown, had developed his multi-slash power by necessity in the earliest, understaffed days of the company, and was permitted to consolidate it by Berry Gordy as a reward for his unwavering loyalty. Gordy may have gotten into the record business to exercise more control over the product he recorded, but this didn't extend to his artists. Smokey was the only one at the company who wielded such power, and pain-in-the-ass Marvin was not a likely choice as the next to break through to that level. Motown didn't mind Gaye writing his heart out, as all songwriters contracted to the company's Jobete Music were encouraged to do, but they brushed off his production aspirations. The guy was difficult enough to get into the studio and on to the road. Why give their biggest-selling male artist one more excuse not to record and tour?

A producer's contract with Motown was not easy to come by in any event. Norman Whitfield had to bang on the door for years before he was finally admitted to the inner circle. Some never were. Sylvia Moy contends that many of the hits on which she has a writer's credit (including Uptight and My Cherie Amour for Stevie Wonder, and It Takes Two for Marvin and Kim Weston) should also list her as a co-producer, but that the company was not ready to welcome a woman into this exclusively gentlemen's club.

"They didn't object to me doing the work," she maintains, "but they did *not* want to give me credit. It was difficult for women in the record industry as a whole then, and at Motown it was just accepted that producers were men. I was so excited when we cut Uptight, but I can't tell you how terrible I felt when I saw the record and my name wasn't on it. I have a stack of memos that say 'no label credit'. It was inter-office paperwork that I wasn't supposed to see, but I got my hands on it. I finally did start getting paid on some, though not nearly all of it. But I don't get credit to this day. Why did I put up with it? Because many of us were people who had been rejected by the big companies. I had been told in New York that I would never be a songwriter. Motown believed in us, and if you made a contribution you got a check every week. That check in your hand told you that you were valued. 'Course, mine was half of what the men got, but still . . ."

Despite all this, Marvin would not be dissuaded. Norman Whitfield, in a rare interview granted to David Ritz, said "I wish I had done more with Marvin. But the truth is that I was the one who told Marvin he didn't need a producer. Most artists can't evaluate themselves, but

Marvin could. He had that kind of taste and detachment. I remember the day in Detroit he invited me to his house on Outer Drive and played some tracks he was about to produce on Sammy Davis Jr. That's when Berry was signing mainstream artists like Sammy and Billy Eckstine. Marvin's stuff for Sammy wasn't commercial, but it was gorgeous. I was stunned. I said, 'Marvin, next time out produce yourself.' 'Why, Norman,' Marvin said, 'that's mighty white of you. That's mighty unselfish.' I was just being honest. The Sammy album never happened, but Marvin never looked back."

Well, not quite. Marvin prepared for the bold leap into the future that was *What's Going On* – or, considering how insulated the Motown kingdom was, perhaps it was more of a bold leap into the present – with a loving look back over his shoulder.

3 For Real

I'm a little mischievous in my music. I like to play.
I want everybody, as long as I'm here, to say 'I
wonder what Marvin is going to do.'

Marvin Gaye

RICHARD MORRIS HAD BARELY GOTTEN TO
sleep in the early morning hours of June 5, 1968 when
he was awakened by a call from Marvin Gaye. Morris
had recently returned to the Motown fold after having
produced hits on Edwin Starr (Headline News, Stop
Her On Sight) and J.J. Barnes (Real Humdinger) for the
rival Ric-Tic Records. He was due in the Snakepit later
that day to cut tracks intended for the Supremes,
Vandellas, and the Gaye/Stover/Gaye song Court Of

The Common Plea for Dennis Edwards. But the singer had more pressing concerns, and urged the producer to come over to his house without delay. Gaye was a few months away from the mega-detonation of Grapevine, but he was still the Prince Of Motown. Morris got up and got dressed.

"I'd known him of course," Morris recalls, "and I'd seen him around Golden World a few times, but we didn't get really tight until he called me and asked if I would help him produce some of his songs. I had a producer's contract, and he wanted to figure out how to put his material together. That worked out well for both of us." Gaye was canny enough not to seek the assistance of producers whose territorialism would be aroused. In April he'd gotten his feet wet on sessions with Ivy Hunter, as much a Motown maverick as Marvin. But in the street-wise, no-nonsense Morris, who had as little trouble standing up to Berry Gordy as Marvin did, he'd found the man who would help him get the job done.

When Morris got to Marvin's house, the singer told him he'd written the song they were looking for. He sat down and played a lovely melody at ballad tempo, then began to sing a lyric of sweet anguish. Its romantic simplicity was designed to accommodate a lush vocal arrangement, making it less a solo vehicle than something he might've sung in his early doo-wop days as a member of Harvey Fuqua's second-generation Moonglows. He called it The Bells, and suggested to Morris that it would be perfect for the Originals, Motown's house backing vocalists who seldom got the opportunity to stand in the spotlight as themselves.

Richard Morris: "He wanted to know how soon we could cut it. I said, 'How 'bout tomorrow?' and got on the phone to Paul Riser. It was probably well beyond 2 am but Paul came over. Marvin played the song, and then hummed some other parts he envisioned while Paul wrote it all down. We talked awhile about the production, and the effect we wanted to achieve. We probably didn't get out of there until four in the morning, but we had it all mapped out. I just added it to my session the following afternoon."

Though it was intended for the Originals, the track they cut that day wound up being vocalised by Bobby Taylor & the Vancouvers. Nobody involved remembers why or how, but my best guess is that, with Taylor riding high on the charts with Does Your Mama Know About Me, the hunt was on for a follow-up and Morris offered The Bells as a possibility. Taylor's vocal dominance wasn't the doo-wop blend Marvin had envisioned, but his was a soulful reading that stood its own ground. When

Richard Morris submitted it at the next creative meeting, however, he got a rude awakening.

"This was the big meeting," Morris remembers of the consolidated gatherings that replaced the old multi-meeting system once Berry Gordy began spending more and more time in the company's Los Angeles office. "There'd be all the producers and writers, but also sales people, secretaries and wannabes, all evaluating songs with Berry running the show. He had a habit of pissing me off. They played The Bells and when it was over Berry asked who'd produced the record. Billie Jean Brown told him it was me. He said, 'That's a terrible song, the track is too slow, that's a horrible ballad. We can't sell stuff like that.' But I knew that his problem wasn't with my production, it was that he knew of Marvin's involvement with me, and the move Marvin was trying to make. The two of them had personal clashes from the day Marvin married his sister Anna. He said he'd talk to me after the meeting. Outside in the hall he said, 'You know, if the lyrics on this song were rewritten I might consider putting it out, even though I really don't like it.' I said 'Man, you know perfectly well who wrote that song, and if he wants to change the lyrics that's up to him. You know who wrote it, you know who produced it, why do you want to put me through these changes?' I was beginning to feel like a guy in the middle of something serious here."

Marvin, however, was surprisingly amenable to the suggestion. Perhaps he had to admit that in this instance Berry was right. The lyric was weak; full of stilted language and clumsy images like lips being "entwined." He quickly worked up another set of lyrics, and Bobby Taylor sang The Bells even more passionately the second time around. This second version, its words different but not noticeably improved, was also rejected. But this was not the end of the road for The Bells. Marvin was still convinced that this song held the key to his aspirations, if only he could find the right focus. When he did, it brought the would-be producer back to the group he'd intended it for all along.

For the Originals, it came not a moment too soon.

When you talk about the quartet that dubbed itself the Originals, you're standing in some of the deepest shadows of Motown. Signed like any other aspiring group, their vocal flexibility soon made them in demand as backing singers on Motown sessions. It also got them typecast as "the background singers", and once you were assigned a cog in the Motown machine it was mighty hard to become anything else. Between the Originals and their distaff equivalent the Andantes they'd sung on literally thousands of records. These guys and gals were on more hits than any other voices on the label, yet they remained the two most obscure groups signed to Motown.

Sylvia Moy: "There are those who'll tell you the Andantes were one of the strongest groups vocally that Motown ever had. They sang on about 80 per cent of the hits Motown put out, so they were more valuable to the company singing backgrounds. Berry had worked the assembly line at the automobile factories, and he knew that things would only run smoothly if everything was in its proper place. So there was no interest in seeing them step forward as a recording group. It was the same for the guys in the Originals."

The Originals' roots at the label actually ran deeper than any act, including Smokey and the Miracles. Future members Walter Gaines and C.P. Spencer were two of the Five Stars, whose 1957 recording of Ooh Shucks was Berry Gordy's first attempt at production. Gaines became the A&R director at Anna Records, the immediate precursor to Tamla-Motown. The fancy title simply meant that he did whatever there was to do, something he continued to do when Anna was folded into Berry Gordy's fledgling operation. "We all worked *so* hard to get this Motown thing started," Gaines recalls. "I'd be there all night long, back in the back room packing records, sending them out to DJs and distributors, or driving around delivering them myself. At the time, I was the only one at the company who had a car. So I was driving Berry, and Berry's whole family; Gwen and all of them. Picking people up at the airport – well, in those days I guess it would've been the train or bus station. We didn't know anybody who could afford to fly."

Gaines also recorded for Anna as a member of the Voicemasters, a group that at various times included Lamont Dozier, Lawrence Payton, David Ruffin, Melvin Franklin, and a fresh off the bus Marvin Gaye. "I met him the first time Harvey Fuqua brought him into Detroit, to perform with the Moonglows [at the Twenty Grand club in late '59]," says Gaines. "He was singing first tenor and had a great harmony voice, but he also had a presence that stood him out from the rest of the group. Off-stage he was kinda shy, didn't take to too many people. He was a loner. He moved around with no specific place to live. He would stay here or there for a couple of weeks, then someplace else for a while. I know how it is coming from out of town, so I kind of took him under my wing. I would take him around to my people, make sure he had good meals and so forth.

"We used him as a studio player at first. He was a self-taught drummer, and he played a pretty fair piano too. In those days you just did whatever you could to become involved. But he always had ambitions to be a pop vocalist, the complete entertainer like Nat Cole. He always would strive for perfection. He wanted to make it, but from the beginning he wanted to make it *his* way. I saw a lot of people shy away from working with him because of his particularities. He didn't want to be just any type of singer."

Walter Gaines was drafted in 1961 and stationed in Germany just as Motown was heating up. "Gwen Gordy was sending me all the records. All these people that I knew from the street – some of them were on welfare when I left – were making hit records. Smokey had a pretty good reputation going, but suddenly here's Mary Wells, the Marvelettes, and all these others. When I heard Stubborn Kind Of Fellow, I couldn't *believe* it was Marvin Gaye, because that was not his type of singing at all." The young singer complained about this when Gaines caught up with him at the Motortown Revue's first performance at the Apollo Theater in New York, but the newness of his commercial success seemed to compensate for the indignity.

Back in Detroit, Gaines recruited former Voice-masters C.P. Spencer and Hank Dixon as part of a new group they called the Originals. "We made a name for ourselves in the clubs," Gaines recalls. "We never dressed alike; each of us would go out there wearing a different colored suit. The Temptations acknowledged that this was something they stole from us. And we never featured one lead singer; we switched all the time." Lamont Dozier suggested Freddie Gorman to complete the lineup. Gorman was another with deep Motown roots. The singer's day job had been the inspiration for the Marvelettes' Please Mr Postman, the company's first Number 1 record. Three years later he was still working at the post office, writing (before H-D-H it had been Holland-Dozier-Gorman) and occasionally recording and looking for that elusive big break. When Motown signed the completed quartet, he and the other three Originals thought they'd gotten it.

Not just yet. For reasons not clear, Clarence Paul, assistant to A&R director Mickey Stevenson, concluded that what the Originals lacked was a lead voice. "We had four leads but they decided we needed a lead singer," says Gorman incredulously. "So they put Joe Stubbs in the group. The Four Tops were doing extremely well, and I guess Levi wanted [the company] to do something for his brother. They'd tried putting him in the Contours, but that hadn't worked out either." Like his brother, Joe Stubbs was blessed with prodigious vocal gifts, having followed

Wilson Pickett as a lead singer in the Falcons. He was not, however, an Original. The dictated partnership lasted only a few months, but with Stubbs on lead for their first single Goodnight Irene, the Originals were effectively reduced to being the backing singers on their own debut! It failed to chart, and it would be two years before they got another shot.

For those artists on the lower rungs of the Motown ladder, getting recorded was only the first part of the problem; the second was *what* you recorded. These could be problems even for groups who'd had hits, as Counsil Gay (no relation) of the Contours explained: "If you were a writer and you were trying to make a name for yourself, who would you write your material for? Certainly not a group who had several failures in a row. It's purely a matter of going with a winner. There were so many male groups at Motown that the competition was very keen. So if your records weren't selling, you were moved to the end of the line when material was written."

The Originals were somewhat insulated from this by the regularity of their session work, but this insulated them from their dreams as well. The group was rescued from session oblivion by Lamont Dozier, their original patron at the label. He put their vocals on an H-D-H track called Suspicion, but nothing came of it. Dozier had always promised his old friends that they'd get the full Holland-Dozier-Holland treatment once his breakneck schedule permitted. He made good on his promise in the spring of '68, and they began working on a prototypical H-D-H hit ditty called We've Got A Way Out Love. At a time when Norman Whitfield was beginning to drape the Temptations in the trappings of psychedelic soul, this song harked back to, and in fact referenced, the classic pop Tempts of It's Growing.

The tracking and vocal sessions went smoothly until the news came in August that the writer/producers were being sued by the company for a level of non-productivity that breached their contract. Holland-Dozier-Holland had initiated a work slowdown in late '67 to protest what they saw as insufficient financial recognition, and this explained in part why it took Lamont so long to get around to the Originals. Then came the early November morning when the quartet woke to find their producers' names splashed across the front page of the newspaper, announcing that Brian Holland, Lamont Dozier and Edward Holland had quit Motown and were countersuing the company for $22 million. Left behind was the unfinished Originals track, which had been waiting on horn, string and some vocal overdubs. Motown went ahead and released this skeletal version anyway, probably for no other reason than to spite the traitorous Holland-Dozier-Holland team. The record immediately stiffed, as it was likely intended to.

You're The One, a Gaye-Stover-Gaye-Hunter composition that was produced by Ivy Hunter with an uncredited assist from Marvin not long before he hooked up with Richard Morris, was the B-side of the stillborn single, and this is where the group reconnected with Gaye. (Marvin had also co-written Need Your Lovin' [Want You Back], the B-side of their first single.) Walter Gaines wasn't the only Original who had a personal history with Marvin. Hank Dixon had known him almost as long. His brother, George W. Dixon of the Spinners, used to shepherd Gaye to their church when Marvin first moved to Detroit from Washington, DC. Motown released a solo single Fred Gorman at the time Marvin's version of Mr Sandman was out, so Mr Postman had frequently crossed paths with Mr Sandman at Hitsville and out on the rounds of DJ hops and promo appearances Motown used to curry favor with the local DJs and groom its young talent.

A few months after their second single's setback, the Originals were summoned to Gaye's spacious ranch-style home at 3067 West Outer Drive. It had been Berry Gordy's until 1967, when the Motown potentate acquired an impressive house on Boston Boulevard that immediately became known as "Gordy Manor". One of Detroit's architectural jewels, the three-storey palace had been built in the 1920s at the then-outrageous cost of $1 million. It featured marble floors, frescoes on the ceilings, a cavernous ballroom complete with bandstand, a gymnasium, swimming pool and movie theater, and Gordy boasted that he was prepared to put as much money into the place as he'd paid for it. The move was heavily symbolic, proclaiming Berry Gordy Jr the King of Detroit. (More astute readers of symbolism, however, would have noted ominously Gordy's purchase of a California residence a matter of months later, a house high in the Hollywood Hills bought from comedian Tommy Smothers.)

Berry bequeathed the Outer Drive house to his sister Anna. This occurred as she and her husband were making up after one of their ever more regular spats, and Marvin spent several thousand dollars renovating the home to reflect the tastes of the reunited lovebirds. (This was an undeniably better investment than the $75,000 dollars he lost on the golf course that same year.) Marvin loved his luxurious new digs; he was particularly fond of the electric drapes that would open and close at the flick of a switch. There was plenty of room for the couple and little Marvin Pentz Gaye III – who, it would finally be revealed by Steve Turner in 1998, was not their own or even adopted, but the calculated product of an Anna-sanctioned union of her husband and her 15-year-old niece Denise Gordy – and the other children of the Gordy clan that became part of their extended family. With Elgie Stover around to help keep the household together, Marvin could interact with his brood or remove himself completely. The house on Outer Drive would bear witness to the deepening depression that engulfed him in the aftermath of Tammi Terrell's collapse, and the creative rebirth that would lift him out of it. There, seated at the white baby grand piano in his sunken living room, Marvin played the Originals the song that would finally give the quartet the recognition that had eluded them for so long. It would be sung to the track of The Bells but the melody had been overhauled and the lyric had been changed completely. It replaced the pleading tone of the previous version with a bold declaration of romantic – and, perhaps for Marvin, creative – worthiness that now bore the title Baby I'm For Real.

"Our habit of switching leads is what gave Marvin the idea that Baby I'm For Real was for us," Walter Gaines says. "He already knew what our individual parts would be, and he began running them down to each of us immediately. He sounded so good himself showing us, that we knew it could be a big record." After a couple more rehearsals, they went right into the studio and cut it.

Where the more experienced Richard Morris had directed the tracking and overdub sessions, the Originals remember Marvin being in charge on the vocal dates. Lead lines were distributed among the singers, and the backing parts used the "blow harmony" technique that Harvey Fuqua had devised to make the Moonglows stand out from the doo-wop pack and passed along to his protégé Marvin Gaye. Each lead voice added a different color, and they were mixed and blended masterfully to culminate in the punchline of the song title. For good measure, Eli Fontaine came in and played a sweet saxophone hook in the beginning and repeated it at the end. A punchline and hooks were precisely what the Bobby Taylor versions lacked, and Baby I'm For Real became the song Marvin had been searching for in The Bells.

(You can spot Marvin's voice in just about every song he produced for the Originals. "There were parts in those songs that nobody could have come up with but Marvin, conceptually and vibe-wise," says Clay McMurray. "He'd say 'here's how I want it' and lay it down. But sometimes nobody could get close to what Marvin had done, so they'd have to keep his." This may explain why, even after he'd won his freedom, he did so little production beyond himself. Would you want to be produced by somebody who could sing every word better than you ever will?)

In an irony they did not yet perceive, the Originals had been booked as stand-ins for Bobby Taylor's Vancouvers on a month-long tour with the Temptations, and promptly forgot all about the session. According to Walter Gaines, "When we returned we ran into Harvey Fuqua and he said, 'Man, I heard that thing you cut. You guys got a hit.' We had no idea what he was talking about until he started singing our parts to us. So we called Marvin, and he played it for us." They were amazed by the final product. "We just listened to the tape over and over," Freddie Gorman reports. "You couldn't just hear it once and walk away. You had to hear it again. At the company all the secretaries just loved it, which is always a good sign."

Unfortunately, the people those secretaries worked for didn't share their enthusiasm. As far as Quality Control was concerned, they already had the Originals record they were looking for. They were so convinced that Green Grow The Lilacs, a lovely piece of pop fluff concocted by the company's vanilla specialist Ron Miller (For Once In My Life, A Place In The Sun), was a hit that they were assembling an album of the group's unreleased sessions around it. Despite persistent lobbying by Marvin and Richard Morris (who was on his way out the Motown door a second time), they would not be swayed by Baby I'm For Real. Eventually they recanted to the extent that the song was added to the album, and sweetened the deal by giving Marvin's tune You're The One its second B-side ride as the flip of the surefire smash Green Grow The Lilacs.

Why they chose to ignore Baby I'm For Real is open to speculation. Lilacs did sound like a legitimate contender in a marketplace that was buying the Fifth Dimension by the bucketload. And it would not been out of competitive character for Berry Gordy to've intended the record as a message to Fifth Dimension manager Marc Gordon, a onetime staff producer in the company's first Los Angeles office, that Motown could do that music every bit as well as he could. But the members of the Originals quickly sensed that there may have been a political dimension to the decision as well.

"There was only one thing that worried me when we started working with Marvin," says Walter Gaines. "He was a rebellious person by nature, and always seemed to be at war with the company. I guess he got in bad with the people in charge of Quality Control, because he could – and would – go over their heads. We'd hear from these people, 'Oh, Marvin, he ain't gonna do nothing.' That was the company line. And Marvin would be telling us, 'Just stick with me, I know what I'm doing.' We were hearing it from both sides."

While it would be easy in hindsight to claim that the Originals were squarely in Marvin's corner, Gaines offers a bluntly honest account of his group's position: "We kept our mouths closed. Our attitude was that, because we'd been working with so many people doing so many different styles, we didn't care *where* it came from. By this time we'd cut sides with Clay McMurray, Lamont Dozier, Ivy Hunter, Frank Wilson, Richard Morris, Ron Miller, even a couple of things with Smokey. We just wanted a hit record, and we would've gone any way they wanted us to go. We were hoping it would be Marvin's tune, though, because we felt he'd done the best job of showing off our voices."

To the surprise of everyone except Marvin Gaye, the surefire rocket Green Grow The Lilacs never got off the launching pad. "They spent a lot of money on that record," Gaines says. "It was so well produced that it could be put out right now and wouldn't sound dated. It just didn't sound like the Originals. The black DJs especially didn't think it was our sound, and wouldn't go near it." When the *Green Grow The Lilacs* album came out five weeks later, its title song was already a dead issue. And so, apparently, was the album. With two stiff singles, the company did not seem inclined to pursue it further.

Shortly thereafter the group was hanging out at local R&B radio powerhouse WCHB. According to Gaines, "We had Detroit sewed up, even without a record. We had a good name from working the clubs and record hops; we had been doing favors for disc jockeys for years. Everybody liked us, and they said, 'We got to get a hit on you guys, but that Lilac record ain't really you.' We were back in the office, and we put Baby I'm For Real on for them. They listened, listened again, and started screaming, 'Man, *this* is the hit.' They called the program director for authorisation, and put it on the air while we were out there. They played it, and then played it over again. Ten minutes later they played it a third time. They played it again while we were driving home. It was an overnight smash in Detroit."

It spread from Detroit like a doo-wop virus, eventually hitting Number 1 on the R&B charts and Number 14 pop. Motown recalled the album and reissued it as *Baby I'm For Real* without changing the cover art. Thirty years later, the CD still shows the title set against a background of green lilac leaves. Without a producer's contract, Marvin's name did not appear on the single. But because Marvin had obviously been intimately involved in the hit,

Motown protocol dictated that he get first crack at the follow-up. Morris had moved on, so this would be his first solo production. The Gaye-Stover-Gaye factory had a song all worked out. It was a lovely little number called The Bells. They'd gone back to the song of the same name sung by Bobby Taylor and, keeping the basic lyric framework, had rewritten and sharpened the words which would be set in a newly recorded track. The only lyric that was retained as-is was a line Bobby Taylor had originally sung, but which would become the spoken interlude in the Originals' revamped version.

The atmosphere around the recording of The Bells was markedly different from the previous single. The Originals finally had a hit, and Marvin had succeeded in producing one. "Our rehearsals were more like social events," Walter Gaines remembers. "We'd go over to his house with our wives and girlfriends, and he'd have it set up like a party. While they ate and drank, we'd be in another room working on the song. Then we'd come out and present what we'd worked out. Marvin liked to try his stuff out on people to see how they'd take to it. 'See what you think of this,' he'd say, and of course our friends and families would be screaming. He didn't have any problem getting company over to his house."

According to Joe Schaffner, on Outer Drive "it was

pretty much an open-door policy. He would buy, like, half a cow and put it in the freezer. I would go out and get cases of liquor. Marvin never drank much, but he had to have 30-year-old Scotch for his guests. It cost a fortune. You could sit down, have a drink, smoke some pot, eat a great meal. You were always made to feel comfortable in his house. So he never had to leave, because everybody would come to him."

Hank Dixon: "But when we got into the studio he was all business. He knew what he wanted everybody to do, and exactly how everything should sound. He was very deliberate; there was a certain way he wanted it, and no other way. Matter of fact, he doubled some of the voices himself, just to get a certain intonation. Sometimes he'd tell you what he wanted and you'd think, 'oh no, this is never gonna work.' But then he'd sing the part to you and you understood how it fit the blend. He was a superb producer of voices." It was a knack Marvin had acquired back in the Moonglows days, when the hungry youngster made a practice of learning the other singers' parts in addition to his own, prompting Harvey Fuqua to deputise him to conduct group rehearsals during the leader's absences. These were musical muscles he hadn't exercised in years, but the day was soon coming when he'd be well served by the workout.

The seeds of a new direction for his own music had been germinating for some time now. Ivy Hunter remembers hearing bits of the future even before Marvin hooked up with the Originals. "He called me to the house because he wanted me to help him with some song ideas he was working on," the producer says. "That day we came up with You're The One, which we cut first on him and then on the Originals. Then he sat at the piano and played me some other ideas he was working on, little pieces of things that sounded strange and extreme. They were a departure from the norm, no doubt about that. I didn't see how he expected to get that sort of stuff ever released, because my stuff was also a departure from the Motown norm, and they were putting it in the can with both hands," the producer laughs. "He was using a lot of unexpected chords, minor 7ths and 9ths, that after *What's Going On* would be identified as Marvin Gaye-type chords. Stevie Wonder also had certain chords he favored, and these things are like fingerprints. You go to a museum and look at Van Gogh and Rembrandt. They're using the same tools, but you have no difficulty telling which is which."

The Bells repeated the success of Baby I'm For Real, peaking at Number 4 R&B and Number 12 pop. Marvin was vindicated. The back-to-back successes with the Originals didn't just establish him as a producer, but as a writer/producer, the Motown ultimate, a director of destinies. The next destiny he would direct was his own.

4 America's Sweethearts

When I learned just how sick she was, I cried. Love
seemed cruel to me. Love was a lie. Tammi was the
victim of the violent side of love – at least that's
how it felt. I have no first-hand knowledge of what
killed her, but it was a deep vibe, as though she was
dying for everyone who couldn't find love. My heart
was broken.

Marvin Gaye

IT WAS ALMOST A RELIEF WHEN TAMMI TERRELL
was finally released from her pain early in the morning of
March 16, 1970. Motown had just released a Marvin Gaye
and Tammi Terrell *Greatest Hits* album, but the hits had
stopped coming for Tammi 18 months earlier. In the

cruellest irony of all, the day of her funeral fell on the American release date of the duo's surprise UK hit The Onion Song, on which the part of Tammi Terrell was impersonated by writer/producer Valerie Simpson. For the record, Simpson has always denied that she took the part in this deception, even after Marvin finally spilled the beans to David Ritz. But there is mounting evidence to suggest that the practice may have been in effect as early as You're All I Need To Get By in the spring of 1968.)

Martha Reeves remembers Tammi showing up at a Vandellas appearance after one of her eight brain operations, bravely trying to put on a good front, but barely able to hold her head up. Then she appeared to rally. "We went to a party and were surprised to see her there," recalled Louvain Demps of the Andantes. Tammi was wrapped in white mink that was said to be a gift from James Brown. "She was upbeat. She told me she was recovering, and that she had made medical history by pulling through. It was the last time I saw her. I gather that not long after this she took a turn for the worse again . . ."

When the inevitable finally happened, Marvin was devastated. By all accounts, it was like something inside him had perished along with his singing partner. "Well before Tammi died, I remember this one particular night he gave me a ride home from a session," says Demps. "I didn't drive and usually took a taxi, but Marvin offered to drive me. There was obviously something weighing on his mind. We sat in front of my house and talked late into the night. He began to tell me how fearful he was that she wasn't gonna make it. There was *such* sadness there. Marvin was a very spiritual man, and he loved her in a spiritual way. He was also the kind of person who could get you to tell him things you might not tell anybody else. My impression was that she confided in him, and he comforted her."

Beneath the shiny vinyl surface of their duets, Tammi Terrell was as complex as Marvin, and no less troubled. Thomasina "Tammy" Montgomery was a sexy, elfin tornado who had lived several lifetimes in her few years. Though technically still a teenager when Berry Gordy spotted her opening for Jerry Butler at the Twenty Grand nightclub in 1965, she was already a battle-scarred veteran of the R&B wars. She was signed by Luther Dixon to Wand Records and backed by the Shirelles when she was only 14. She'd toured as part of James Brown's Revue and recorded for his Try It label. At the time Gordy encountered her, she was coming off a brief association with Chess Records, though not, as has been claimed, a brief marriage to heavyweight boxer Ernie Terrell.

However the name was acquired, Tammy Montgomery arrived in Detroit reborn as Tammi Terrell.

Though the Motortown machinery produced an abundance of home-grown talent, the company would occasionally let down the drawbridge to admit an unfulfilled veteran or a promising unknown. Both descriptions fit Tammi Terrell. Among her closest friends at the company was another outsider, the Los Angeles-based Brenda Holloway. "I don't care for the word 'outsiders,'" Miss Holloway demurs. "I thought of us as the *adopted* children, because Berry went out and picked us to be included within the company family. Tammi and I bonded immediately because we were both adopted Motown children."

They were greeted by a sea of smiling faces, but it was not exactly the happy playground of Motown myth. When Tammi arrived and was lavished with what was perceived to be special attention (including a complete makeover in the dental department) and then began a torrid affair with Temptations leading man David Ruffin, there was resentment from those who'd been dutifully standing in line waiting to have the magic wand finally waved over *their* heads.

"Tammi and I both felt that we needed to align with each other," says Holloway. "We were all young, and there was a lot of rivalry, like female sibling rivalry. It was all within the female groups and singers, though the men probably had the same thing going. It wasn't anything we introduced to the situation; it was there when we arrived. The company was small in the early days, and Berry Gordy couldn't make us all stars at the same time. Everybody was trying to get into that key spot, the Mary Wells position. When she left, the Supremes fit right in. Everybody else was trying to get into that next-in-waiting seat. Everybody was fighting – well not so much fighting as competing, to get as close as possible. Tammi never talked about people, but she was alarmed by the jealousy of the women at Motown. But Tammi was a free spirit, she didn't really care what people said or thought of her. Tammi was always protecting other people – like me, because I was less experienced at dealing with this sort of thing – instead of protecting herself.

"She was bound to attract that sort of jealousy, just because she was so glamorous. Tammi was sexually appealing. She was *very* sexy, the sexiest woman at Motown. They talked about me on those terms too, but my appeal had more to do with my body. She was a Marilyn Monroe sexy, because she didn't really know – a little girl quality, an instinctive sexiness. It was also wrapped up in her desire to please as an entertainer. But that free spirit part was something men felt the need to try and control, and that always created problems. She was very bold; she had what it took to be a star. She didn't have the greatest voice, but she had a style you couldn't miss. Tammi had that flair that commands your attention. Ultimately I think she would have gone into acting, and it wouldn't surprise me if maybe Mr Gordy didn't have some thoughts in that direction, once he dealt with his other . . . priorities."

Elgie Stover: "She was cool. She was the highlight of any Motown gathering, a real firecracker. Sure, she was a little wild, but she was well-educated. The girl had studied psychology! She taught Marvin a lot about how to handle himself, without him even being aware of it. She was an enlightening person. Her personality and lifestyle were different from everyone else at Motown. She came from the outside, but I thought she was on her way to being a real trendsetter. In her mind, the records with Marvin were just the beginning."

But there was another, darker side to Tammi Terrell. "I often think of her as a Michael Jackson in that she had no childhood," says Brenda Holloway. "She started entertaining when she was very, very young. When you miss out on your childhood it's like a piece of the puzzle is permanently lost, and you have no idea how to find it.

Tammi was looking for that little girl part, because she'd always had to be a woman. So she looked for men to fix it, companions to fix it, career to fix it, potions to fix it. I was like that myself, until one day I sat down and took the time to discover that I'm OK without any of those things. For many years I was terrified of being by myself in a room. Tammi was like that; she didn't want to be alone with Tammi.

"She started on a bad foundation. I don't quite know how to express it, and I don't want to get into anything legal, but her bad experiences were while she was touring with James Brown. Part of the bad foundation – and a part of womanhood – is thinking we need a man to validate us. James Brown did validate Tammi in her professional life, because he gave her a chance. But in her personal life he messed her up. She lost a lot of self-esteem, a lot of spirit. She was a free spirit, but when she came to Motown a part of her was wounded. She had a sadness like Marvin had, that you could feel through the glamorous exterior. She came to Motown to be healed, to start over, and I think that's what the name change was about."

Any threat the other women of Motown may have felt did not materialise immediately. The first few singles released after she signed with the company in 1965 only scraped the charts. In fact, until she was paired with Marvin Gaye in early 1967, Tammi Terrell had not come close to delivering on the promise Berry Gordy saw in her. The fairytale pairing with David Ruffin had likewise started with high hopes, but devolved into a series of public spats and clashes. Then there were the headaches. A minor annoyance at first, their frequency and strength eventually increased beyond the reach of over-the-counter painkillers, and she resorted to stronger medications. Some of the cattier women intimated that this was no more than a plea for attention by a diva whose records weren't happening, but the pain was all too real.

Brenda Holloway: "My belief is that it came from injuries she'd sustained in her past as Tammy Montgomery, and that these had weakened her. You can paint a house that's condemned and live in it, but you just know the first big storm that comes along will make it cave in. When Berry got her, the foundation had already been established. The pattern was set. I remember her beginning to complain about the headaches. Knowing her, I have no doubt that she'd been suffering with them for awhile before that. Then on my next trip to Detroit she had a bag, and I mean a *shopping bag*, full of prescription bottles, because she didn't know which pill was going to ease her terrible pain. After a while, none of them did."

When these persistent headaches culminated in the October 1967 on-stage collapse, the rumor swept through Motown that her boyfriend, the equally volatile David Ruffin, had inflicted the damage with a hammer. This ugly bit of Motown lore has never been substantiated, but another story that had an enraged Ruffin pushing Terrell down a flight of stairs was apparently accurate. "She told me herself that's what had happened," says Elaine Jesmer, who authored the 1973 Motown *roman à clef* Number One With A Bullet featuring characters based on both Tammi and Marvin. "She said that she and James Brown had gotten into it too. Tammi had quite a history. She'd paid her dues long before she arrived at Motown. Tammi prided herself on the fact that she could kick David's ass as hard as David kicked hers. That's the way she looked at it. But that's not the issue here. They [Motown] knew something was wrong. They had people traveling with her – that she was paying for, by the way – and none of them ever thought to get her to a doctor. 'Oh, she's just doing too many drugs.' I can't tell you how many times I heard that. It may or may not have been true, but she didn't get brain cancer from doing too many drugs. She was trying to deaden a very real pain, and nobody picked up on that."

*

It is Brenda Holloway's view, however, that Tammi wouldn't necessarily have heeded the warning signals had they been correctly interpreted. "She'd been having these headaches and not telling anybody," her friend says. "Tammi's personality was always the quick fix. She just wanted to feel better so she could get on with the right-now, where all free spirits live. When she teamed with Marvin and finally began to see the success she'd been working toward since she was five years old, she wasn't about to slow down for anything."

For these two troubled souls, the time Marvin Gaye and Tammi Terrell spent together as America's Sweethearts was something more than playacting. Certainly for Marvin, and possibly Tammi as well, the musical relationship was a safe haven in which the romantic fairytale sentiments of songs like Your Precious Love and You're All I Need To Get By were as true for the singers as for the sung-to. Every time their voices came together, they connected with an empathy so profound that no other word but love adequately describes it.

It happened the very first time their voices met, and they weren't even in the room together. Marvin arrived at the studio one day in late January 1967 to nail down his end of a new duet pairing the company had devised in the wake of Kim Weston's departure from

Motown with her husband Mickey Stevenson just as her duet with Marvin, It Takes Two, was taking off. Gaye had only a passing acquaintance with Tammi Terrell and had little idea what she sounded like. He was scheduled to cut his half of the vocals on the first contribution of the young writing team of Nick Ashford and Valerie Simpson, who had composed Let's Go Get Stoned for Ray Charles before Berry Gordy lured them from New York to the Motor City.

When producers Harvey Fuqua and Johnny Bristol heard the demo of Ain't No Mountain High Enough, they felt they had the breakthrough song for Tammi Terrell that had thus far eluded them. They cut the track, which did not stray far from Ashford and Simpson's blueprint, in December '66. Tammi's vocals and the strings were added in early January. Then Berry Gordy had a very bright idea. We don't know whether it was because It Takes Two was set to become Marvin's biggest duet yet and he had nothing to follow it with, or because he wanted to send a message to Mickey and Kim that anybody was quickly replaceable, or just because he had a creative hunch, but Berry Gordy's sudden decision that the voice of Marvin Gaye should be added to make Ain't No Mountain High Enough a duet was among the most radiant moves of his brilliant career. It was obvious to all present on January 29 when Marvin began replacing selected lines of Tammi's with his own. Even in this artificial setting – not at all unusual at Motown, where grueling schedules frequently dictated that duets be pieced together – they sparked and sparkled.

Johnny Bristol: "They were perfectly matched in the blend of their tonalities. Tammi's voice was very light in comparison with Marvin's other singing partners, and when it met up with his easy style there was a brightness to the combination that just sounded like romance. It was a once in a lifetime connection of voices."

This was confirmed when Your Precious Love, also from Ashford and Simpson's demo reel, surpassed the smash Ain't No Mountain High Enough and made Marvin hotter as a duet partner than he was as a solo singer. (This would remain the case until Grapevine made him double dynamite at the end of '68, a one-two punch unmatched by any other Motown artist.) They sang face-to-face the second time around, and it showed. On Ain't No Mountain all the ad-libs had been Marvin's, as he masterfully wove his voice around Tammi's existing track to create the illusion of a duet. But listen to the difference between Terrell's singing there and her second verse of Your Precious Love. In the physical presence of her partner her vocal becomes playful, flirtatious; it is the illusion of Ain't No Mountain High Enough made flesh.

As the two spent time together as people they discovered something more valuable than hit records. They were lost soulmates who offered an emotional comfort to each other that neither found easy to come by elsewhere. "They were at their happiest and at their best when they were together as a team," believes Brenda Holloway. "Marvin and Tammi were a true *team* – both extraordinary people who reached another level when you put them together. Marvin had become known for a more driving sound, but here he was able to kick back and relax. Tammi made Marvin feel safe enough that he could take off his armor around her. You felt a little lighter, a little more comfortable, when Tammi was around. She helped me relax too, because I was always a little tense. If you accepted her for who she was, she could really help you. She was not just a beautiful woman; as a person she was a soothing balm."

The series of records they made together – first with Fuqua and Bristol, then with Ashford and Simpson producing as well as writing – set an emotional standard for pop duet singing that remains without peer. Marvin Gaye and Tammi Terrell had a musical relationship that was to pop what the combination of Billie Holiday and Lester Young had been to jazz – perfectly matched instruments that brought out the best in each other. It also pulled If This World Were Mine out of Gaye, one of his loveliest songs and a rare solo composition. Though their time together would be measured in months, what they achieved stands beyond time.

Where they truly came to life was on stage. The two played lovers to perfection, with plenty of their own personalities brought to the roles. "She loved to embarrass him up there," Elaine Jesmer remembers. "*Loved it.* It was kind of hilarious. She'd get right up in his face and flirt with him, and he didn't have a clue how to handle this. She was much more sophisticated than he was. Marvin was so vulnerable in those days, sweet and kind of spacey, and he didn't have a clue how to handle this. He looked so embarrassed that you had to laugh. She was much more sophisticated than he was, and *really* enjoyed pulling his chain. He enjoyed it too, but I think Marvin was slightly scared of her at the same time. And I think she liked it that way."

When Tammi could no longer perform on stage, Marvin fulfilled a few contractual obligations with Barbara Randolph and a singer named Ann Bogan. "She went on-stage and tried to outsing him," Elgie Stover says of the latter somewhat ruefully, as Bogan was drafted at his suggestion. "She tried to steal the show! She was a church girl, and she got a little too happy. She went jumpin' and hoppin' across that stage like Patti Labelle, and then she got to shoutin'. She just left him standing there, looking around."

No replacement, however sympathetic, would have been up to this task. Nobody was Tammi, nobody could be, and Gaye announced that he would never sing with another partner. Ever the fighter, Tammi hung in there a little longer in the studio, continuing to hold up her end even after her first couple of unsuccessful surgeries. When she died in March 1970 she hadn't sung for well over a year, and the *Marvin Gaye & Tammi Terrell Greatest Hits* album released by Motown that same month contained three of the tracks on which Valerie Simpson had impersonated her. The last genuine Marvin and Tammi hit released before she went home to Philadelphia for good was called Keep On Lovin' Me Honey.

For a hopeless romantic like Marvin, what was lost with Tammi's passing was a purity that existed nowhere else in his life, a purity that was maintained because – despite the suspicions of Anna Gordy Gaye – the relationship never crossed the line and became physical.

"Marvin and Tammi had a relationship that was unique unto itself," declares their road manager Joe Schaffner. "She was a streetwise girl, and Marvin liked girls who were a little wild. He had a love affair with her, but it was in his mind. What they shared was the closeness of two people who truly liked each other. They would often have to share dressing rooms, which meant that you watched each other dress and undress. It was like having his own private show, this very sexy woman changing her clothes in front of him. He could have all the lust in his heart that he wanted, but he wasn't going to do anything about it. He admired her from a distance. They were *not* lovers. They could sleep in the same bed and never ever do anything. That's the way it was. For one thing he was too chicken to make any moves, David Ruffin known for being as crazy as he surely was. But that wasn't gonna be the nature of it anyway. Marvin and Tammi had a pure friendship, what we'd call soulmates today."

That Marvin and Tammi never became lovers, and that they channeled that energy into their performances together, is a lovely romantic image to place atop their make-believe wedding cake. It is wisdom that everyone I spoke to accepted as gospel, at least until I spoke to her friend Brenda Holloway, who chuckled when I ran the party line by her. "Only Tammi Terrell and Marvin Gaye know for sure. *Only* Marvin and Tammi. Put that in your book," she says with a sly laugh.

There was no laughter the last time she saw

Tammi. "It was just before they sent her back to Philadelphia. She was in a terrible, terrible state. The stardom and all that other stuff fell away, because Tammi was sick and didn't know what to do. But I think she always knew more about her condition than she let on, and this is before the surgeries. She probably knew what was happening; when death is around, people know. When I saw her she was shaking. She knew. And it wasn't that Motown turned its back on her. They didn't. What hurt the most was when they had to tell her she simply wasn't able to sing anymore. Then she was Tammy Montgomery again."

Obie Benson: "We saw her when the Four Tops played in Cherry Hill, New Jersey. Her mother brought her; she was in a wheelchair by then. She had done her best to get fixed up, but you could tell she was having a hard time. Still, she was beautiful even then. She hugged us and told us she loved us. I said, 'OK, baby, we'll see you next time we come back.' She just gave me this sad little smile. Two weeks later she was gone."

At her funeral in Philadelphia on March 20, Marvin appeared to have sailed over the edge emotionally, babbling sadly and talking to the deceased as if she could answer him. After the funeral, Marvin withdrew to the sanctuary of the house on Outer Drive, and refused to come out and play on any level. No recording. no touring, and the few contacts with the company were carried out by go-betweens like Elgie Stover and Joe Schaffner. But his retreat was not entirely without purpose. He had been presented with a song that would, at least for a while, restore some balance to his troubled life.

5 What's Happening, Brother?

If my emotions or feelings say I shouldn't do some-
thing because of a very strong principled position
that I must take, then in spite of the consequences,
in spite of all that is facing me from a detrimental
point of view, then I have to remain true to my
artistic nature.

Marvin Gaye

RENALDO "OBIE" BENSON OF THE FOUR TOPS
had never been a particularly prolific songwriter, but
something began to percolate during a tour stop in San
Francisco that coincided with violent skirmishes between
protesters and Berkeley police over a disused urban lot
called People's Park. "They had the Haight-Ashbury then,"

he recalls, "all the kids up there with the long hair and everything. The police was beatin' on them, but they weren't bothering anybody. I saw this, and started wondering what the fuck was going on. What is happening here? One question leads to another. Why are they sending kids so far away from their families overseas? Why are they attacking their own children in the streets here? And so on." With the help of lyricist Al Cleveland, who worked frequently with Smokey Robinson and rented the upstairs of Obie's duplex, Benson began shaping a song that addressed these issues.

The Four Tops, however, weren't interested in it. "My partners told me it was a protest song. I said no, man, it's a love song, about love and understanding. I'm not protesting, I want to know what's going on. But they never really understood what was happening." When the group toured England, Benson thought he'd stumbled on to an interesting match. "We were doing a TV show, Top Of The Pops or one of those, and I tried to give it to this girl. This famous folksinger, played a guitar. What's her name? I went into her dressing room, picked up her guitar and played this song. I had some words, but they weren't the finished lyrics yet. She seemed interested, but somehow we got separated and I never got to finish presenting it to her. What was her name?"

Fate had in mind someone other than Joan Baez to deliver the finished What's Going On.

The only problem was that when Obie took the song to the right singer, Marvin Gaye didn't hear it for himself. He wanted to cut it on the Originals. The oft-repeated story that the progressive song had been written for such a traditional vocal group had always struck this chronicler as improbable, and Benson confirms that this was not the case. "Marvin was the perfect artist for it," he says. "Marvin already felt like this. He was a rebel, and a real spiritual guy. The first time he sang it, I was playing guitar and he was playing piano, and it was so beautiful. I don't know what he heard in it for the Originals, but I finally put it to him like this: I'll give you a percentage of the tune if you sing it, but if you do it on anybody else you can't have none of it. His wife told him, 'Marvin this is a perfect song for you.' I'll love Anna forever for making him see the truth of that."

When Gaye was persuaded to keep it for himself, he not only accepted a percentage of the song, he earned it. "Marvin definitely put the finishing touches on it," Benson readily concedes. "He added lyrics, and he added some spice to the melody. He fine-tuned the tune, in other words. He added different colors to it. He added some things that were more ghetto, more natural, which made it seem more like a story than a song. He made it visual. He absorbed himself to the extent that when you heard that song you could see the people and feel the hurt and pain. We measured him for the suit and he tailored the hell out of it."

The Motown assembly line was ready to provide plenty of assistance with the tailoring. "We used to call it going to work at the factory," recalls keyboard player Johnny Griffith. "One of the secrets of the Motown success was owning their own studios. The studio ran 24 hours a day, with shifts of engineers. It was a three shift operation; that's why we called it the factory."

The original facility in the Hitsville building on West Grand Boulevard was Studio A, better known as the Snakepit, where the basic tracks were cut. (It was called the pit because the studio, in a cinderblock extension built by the previous owner as a darkroom for his photographic business, was reached by a flight of steps down from the control room. The "snakes" were the tangled cords that sprouted from the electric instruments.) "The secret of the so-called 'Motown Sound' was room identity," reckons Hank Cosby. "The drums sat in the same place for years; nothing was ever disturbed. If you moved any of the instruments a couple of feet in either direction it would have changed the sound completely."

Cosby's statement has the ring of truth, but still the Motown Sound eludes pin-down by any single element. In Berry Gordy's compartmentalised assembly line, something essential to that sound was added at each successive stage. To writer/producer Richard Morris, for example, it was the sound of a beat-up old piano: "Downstairs in the basement of Hitsville was where the producers and songwriters had, like, a common room. All of us used to sit around a piano and take turns playing our material. We'd listen to each other's songs, criticise them, trade chords, helping one another develop them without any of the ugly competition that came in later. That's why Motown records had such a continuity of sound at one time. It was there even before it got to the studio musicians, because it all came from that one piano."

One studio eventually proved insufficient to handle the traffic, so in late '67 Berry Gordy set his sights on the acquisition of Golden World Records. It was a deal that would make sense on several levels. Detroit in those years was home to countless little R&B record companies in the shadow of Hitsville, but labels like Fortune, D-Town and LuPine flew too low to even register on the Motown radar. Eddie Wingate's Golden World operation, however, was a legitimate contender. They'd scored hits with Edwin Starr, J.J. Barnes, the Fantastic Four and the instrumental San Remo Golden Strings. Many of Wingate's best records featured moonlighting Motown musicians, and his writing, recording and production operation was a mini-version of Berry Gordy's. In a lightning strike, Gordy rang in New Year 1968 by acquiring the whole package – artists, writers, masters and, most crucially, the piece of real estate called Golden World Studios – for a reported one million pre-inflation dollars. Gordy had eliminated his major local competitor, solved his studio problem and strengthened his artist roster, all in a single swoop. It let everybody in Detroit know in no uncertain terms who was, and intended to remain, the boss.

The spacious Golden World facility became Motown Studio B, perfect for orchestration, vocals and an assortment of other overdubs, even as the house band continued to crank out tracks at Studio A over on the Boulevard. After tracking and overdubbing, the action would then shift to the two studios on the ninth and tenth floors of the new Motown building on Woodward Avenue for mixing. (The original mixes had come out of a small space in the basement of Hitsville, and the new studios were supplemented by a mix room upstairs at Golden World.) There were often times when these facilities weren't enough, and they had to farm out the overflow to other area studios. In a city built on hard work, the factory aspect was something to be celebrated – one early ad proudly proclaimed the company "Detroit's other world-famous assembly line." To keep the line running smoothly required multiple staffs of musicians, arrangers, producers and engineers. In just trying to keep up with itself, Motown assembled a creative team of a depth unmatched by any recording company before or since.

The studio musicians who called themselves the Funk Brothers, first under the leadership of Joe Hunter and then Earl Van Dyke, have begun in recent years to receive a belated fraction of the recognition due them. (As this is written, shooting has been completed on a film documentary based on Standing In The Shadows Of Motown, Allan Slutsky's pioneering book on bassist supreme James Jamerson and the other Brothers.) There was no shortage of supplementary players, but the core team as it evolved under pianist/organist Van Dyke included Jamerson, drummer Benny Benjamin (with backup from Uriel Jones and Richard "Pistol" Allen), guitarists Robert White, Joe Messina and Eddie Willis (which they called the oreo guitar section because the white Messina sat between his two black colleagues), Johnny Griffith on keyboards, and percussionists Jack

Ashford, Eddie "Bongo" Brown and Jack Brokensha (Ashford was Black Jack and Brokensha was White Jack, for self-evident reasons). The Funk Brothers were perhaps the most potent weapon in Berry Gordy's arsenal. He kept them his secret weapon by never crediting their contributions, and he had no intention of sharing their services with anybody.

Uriel Jones: "When I first started doing sessions at Motown, we were getting $5 a tune. Later it went up to $10. Then Ed Wingate over at Golden World started calling, and he'd pay us $20. This was before we started getting union scale and were put on the payroll [at $1000 per week]; then we were making some decent money. Once we got on salary, though, if we get caught working for Wingate or anybody else, we'd be fined $300. See, they had guys taking pictures of us coming out of other people's studios. They'd call us into the office the next day and ask us if we'd done a session for so-and-so. If we said no, they'd throw the pictures on the table. You were busted, and it cost you."

Jack Ashford had no illusions: "There were a lot of musicians hanging around, jockeying for position. The lobby was always full of musicians. If you dropped dead, you knew they'd pull you out of the way and somebody would be there to take your place before the seat was cold. But that was good too, because it made you wood-shed and stay on top of your game. And believe me, man, we were the top."

The only outside Funk Brothers work Berry sanctioned was for Artie Fields, who ran the city's largest commercial studio and produced TV adverts for "The Big Three" automakers – Ford, General Motors and Chrysler – and many other national accounts. Fields discovered that the musical camaraderie developed in the Snakepit was as beneficial to his television commercials as it was to Motown's pop records. "What you have to realise," Fields says, "is that these were accomplished musicians who wound up at Motown because that's what paid the bills. They were capable of playing anything I'd throw at them. We'd write some basic parts out, then stand back as they did their personal stuff that *really* made it happen. Any charts were just a roadmap. Anything more would have been presumptuous with musicians of their caliber. Earl Van Dyke was an extremely versatile piano player. But if he didn't like a producer he'd give him nothing but lounge-style piano. We got along great, but he ran that on two or three of my guys until I'd have to go out into the studio and say 'C'mon, Earl, please ... for me ...'"

The Funk Brothers' primary asset as a band was not the well-drilled precision of R&B – though this is what they achieved as a byproduct – but the internal communication endemic to jazz musicians. The remarkable empathy these players developed was due in large part to their shared roots in modern jazz, chops they maintained by jamming into the wee hours at local clubs after they'd put in a full day on Motown's pop-soul assembly line. These men lived through their instruments. As professional musicians, they did whatever they had to do to survive. Typical of their experience before Motown gave them a stable home was Joe Messina, who had played both with the genius Charlie Parker and the comedian Soupy Sales.

Marvin didn't do any further session or road drumming once his singing career took off. He posed no threat to Benny, Uriel or Pistol to begin with, though he did have the distinction of bringing two members into the Funk Brothers fold. Bongo Brown had been Marvin's valet before his percussion virtuosity earned him a permanent studio spot. And though it's not generally known, it was Marvin Gaye who introduced Jack Ashford into the Brotherhood as well.

"Marvin took me to Motown," the percussionist confirms. "We met in Boston. He stopped into a club where I was appearing with a jazz organ group led by Johnny 'Hammond' Smith. He was impressed with my vibes playing, and had one of his people ask if I'd be interested in joining his road band. He was standing right there, but I had no idea who he was and said 'Never heard of him'. That was the jazz attitude of the time; we were all trying to be cooler than Miles Davis. Because he wasn't singing jazz, I wouldn't have had any interest in what he was doing. He thought it was funny that I'd never heard of him, or Motown either." Still, they exchanged phone numbers. A couple of months later he got a call from Harvey Fuqua, and Ashford was financially persuaded to join Gaye's band on vibes, tambourine and Latin percussion.

"I quickly found out about his strong appreciation of jazz," Black Jack says. "Marvin made it very clear that he did not want to be singing Hitch Hike and those things. That wasn't who he was. He liked to sing Nat King Cole songs. On the tour – at least in the beginning – there was a segment of the show where they'd put a stool out for him, and I'd push the vibes up and comp behind him while he sang Unforgettable and a couple other standards. That segment got dropped fast because, though he sang those songs very well, he was putting his audience to sleep. Marvin would say, 'Man, I sure wish they'd accept it. That's what I really want to do.' I said 'I understand that, but we need to get paid too. Where do you think I am? I'm used to playing Boplicity and Round Midnight and now I'm sitting up here behind you while you sing this shit that you hate."

Ashford needn't have worried. Once they got back to Detroit and he was introduced to the crew in the Snakepit, he never went on the road again. He was a Funk Brother, and became as integral to the rhythmic thrust of the band as James Jamerson and Benny Benjamin. If there is such a thing as the genius of the tambourine – and too many Motown classics to list insist that there is – then Jack Ashford is it. "He was probably the world's greatest percussion player," says percussion partner Jack Brokensha. "He's a huge guy, with hands like big legs of lamb. On tambourine he was amazing; he could sound like a whole rhythm section. A lot of the feel of the tracks was down to the originality of his tambourine and James Jamerson's bass."

The excellence of the musicians is there for all to hear, but their role in shaping the music is still not properly acknowledged. "The musicians had the strongest input in a lot of those Motown songs," states Johnny Griffith. "Most of the producers won't admit how much they depended on us. They'd come in with a *thought*; they'd have a couple of chords and call that a song. We'd sit there and let 'em pound around for awhile, then we'd look at the clock and see that it was time to get moving. We'd say, 'Let's put this together so we can get out of here.' Then everybody would start thinking, and out of that the song would develop. We put a lot of those songs together ourselves, though we never got credit for it. The producers or the guy who wrote the lyrics would be standing up taking all the bows, but so much of that stuff never would have happened without the musicians."

This is caught perfectly in a story told to Jack Ryan by the late Earl Van Dyke: "Berry Gordy's brother George came downstairs one day to produce some material," the bandleader said. "He took the attitude that we didn't understand what he wanted, and he started giving us orders. We had been recording Motown music for quite some time, and this was George's first attempt at producing a record, so we decided to have some fun with him. Instead of putting anything special into the session, we played exactly what was put in front of us. George couldn't understand why the sound he wanted wasn't coming out on the record. After several hours, he called us all together and asked what the problem was. We told him to go into the control booth and leave us alone and we would record the material. In the next hour we recorded four songs exactly the way he wanted. It was our way of showing him that we knew our business and could deliver almost anything a producer wanted, if he showed us some respect."

Hank Cosby: "Half the guys that came here weren't producers until they'd been here two or three years. They had limited musical backgrounds, and had to learn from the musicians what to do and how it was done. Most of them would just sing, and they'd want you to put music to what they were singing. Norman Whitfield didn't know much about music at all, but he became one of the hottest producers in the business. When Holland-Dozier-Holland came through the door they could barely play the piano. But when they left, man, they could *really* play."

Though Andrew Loog Oldham didn't arrive at Motown until later, when the company's ill-conceived white rock label Rare Earth was launched while Berry Gordy was otherwise engaged on the Coast, the former Rolling Stones manager/producer found the machinery functioning with its vaunted precision. "I had never seen a system like it," he says. "I came in to do violins one day and they told me I was up fourth. I asked what they meant by 'up fourth.' They said, 'Well we've got Tom Baird doing 30 pieces, then David Van De Pitte is using 20, and Paul Riser needs 16. You only have eight strings so you're up last, when we've let all the other musicians go.' One could see the wonderful clockwork discipline that was still intact."

The Gordy assembly line was compartmentalised, each cog functioning independently from the next but in synchronous harmony with it. There were disadvantages to the isolation of the individual parts, but it did encourage a system of fraternities to develop. Each compartment boasted its own version of the Funk Brothers. Ed Wolfrum is an engineer who started out at Hitsville, then went on to work at both Golden World and United Sound. "Mike McLean was the head engineer at Motown and the guy responsible for building the studio on the Boulevard," Wolfrum explains. "He had a good-sized boat, a cruiser, and he'd invite a gang of engineers out for an afternoon on the water. Not just Motown but from all the Detroit studios. We called it The Audio Recording & Drinking Society, and we'd have a nice day of socialising, lunch, maybe get up on the waterskis. One afternoon we pulled in at Sinbad's, a restaurant on the river and happened to dock next to [Motown executive] Harry Balk's boat. When he looked over and saw all of us, he chewed us out on the spot: 'Don't ever let me see you together like this again. I don't mind if you socialise, but if something happened to you out on that boat you'd cripple the recording industry in Detroit.' None of us had given this a thought on a business level, that we were an investment to be protected. We were just engineers and friends.

We weren't seeing the larger picture, and I doubt very much that it was ever intended that we should."

Sometimes this isolation of the parts could negatively impact the whole. "There were very few producers who had control over their records past the basic recording," according to Ivy Joe Hunter. "Your product went to Quality Control and if they heard merit in it they'd send it down for what we called 'mastering', which meant the final mix. Often it would be mixed by what they considered to be the Motown Sound. They would modify what you'd done to sound more like whatever else was coming out of the company, which might be an entirely different philosophy from the way the record was cut. I had a real serious problem with the way they mixed a tune that Stevie Wonder and I had recorded on the Four Tops, Loving You Is Sweeter Than Ever. They destroyed it in the mix. Little things you need to hold it together were left out completely because they didn't conform to that week's Motown Sound. Most of the time you wouldn't even hear the final mix until the record was on the street."

After the Funk Brothers, the most unsung part of the process was the contribution of the arranging department. It was the arranger's job to interact between the producers and the musicians, a job whose parameters tended to change with every producer, and then write any horn and string charts. Most of the artists had little or no idea who these people were. "We were not encouraged to be at the studio except for our tracking and sweetening sessions," says arranger David Van De Pitte. "We never came in for the vocals, which meant that we had very little interaction with the artists. I did some great records on Gladys Knight for Johnny Bristol, and she'd never seen my face! I didn't meet her until years later. I went up and introduced myself, and she was astounded. She said, 'You're the guy who did all that wonderful music for me! All those records and we never even met . . .'"

Under the administration of Hank Cosby, the arranging staff at this time included Paul Riser, Wade Marcus, Willie Shorter and the man who was in line to arrange Marvin Gaye's next session, David Van De Pitte.

"They must have had 75 producers, at least 150 songwriters, and *God only knows* how many artists," Van De Pitte says, shaking his head at the enormity of the enterprise. "And us four arrangers were responsible for cranking out all the music that came out of there. We did so much music that it was nuts; we were all going crazy, working non-stop. As long as you could keep your eyes open and a pencil in your hand, you were writing. Mind you, there were two arranging departments. Ours was the recording arranging department. There was a completely separate department to take what we'd done on record and sort of boil it down and rewrite the charts for the road bands. Gil Askey, who was an incredible writer, headed the touring arranging department, and he had Gene Keys, Johnny Allen, who would go on to do Shaft with Isaac Hayes, and H.B. Barnum, who for years functioned in a similar capacity for Aretha Franklin.

"There was a point when I must have been doing two – maybe two and a half – albums' worth of material a week. A week. Wade Marcus had gone off to study Schillinger for awhile, and Willie Shorter had gotten ill. That left Paul and I as the two guys in the arranging department working. They brought in a couple of outside people. Jerry Long would come in from LA periodically. He claimed to have studied with Nadia Boulanger, but who didn't? My dog studied with Boulanger. Jerry could be a great writer – he arranged Just My Imagination for the Tempts – but he was erratic and sometimes difficult to find. So it was basically on Paul and I to do all the work, and it got *raggedy*. Then Wade returned, Willie got somewhat better, and we finally got back to our customary level of overwork and craziness. That was about the time I was summoned by Marvin."

Prodded by the song Obie Benson had dropped in

his lap, Marvin's narrow focus on the Originals was giving way to a widescreen vision of what his own next project would be. It had been spurred by several conversations with his younger brother Frankie, who'd survived a three-year tour of duty in Vietnam. Like so many vets "back in the world" ('Nam lingo for post-combat life), Frankie was haunted by what he'd seen and done. Back home, his sacrifice for his country was rewarded with disdain, disrespect and unemployment. When he could find work, it was as a dishwasher or a doorman.

"Me and Marvin used to play GI Joe all the time as kids," Frankie told me in a soft voice that eerily recalls his older brother's. We spoke only a few days after the death of his father, Marvin Pentz Gay Sr, but the passing of the man who will be remembered more for the taking of a life than for giving it has freed Frankie Gay to reflect. "We played all the 'shoot 'em up' games of children," he says, "cowboys and Indians, cops and robbers, all that stuff. He was a better cowboy, but I was a pretty good Indian. Like a lot of people, Vietnam didn't become real until somebody close to him was touched by it. I wrote him a few letters, but it wasn't 'til I got back that it really hit him that I had been over there. 'Wow, man, you were in the *war*.' Then he wanted to know everything.

"I cried a lot during our talks. War *is* hell, believe

me. The value of life is unbelievably low. Nothing you've ever experienced can prepare you for the terror. And the blood; all my memories of that time are swimming in blood. This horrified Marvin, but what moved him most was the image of children eating out of garbage cans. That was hard for him to get past. It's a sight that I don't think anybody wants to see: people – *children* – trying to live off what you throw away. Our garbage cans were always clean. When I saw that, I always tried to leave some food on my plate so that they would have something to eat. A lot of other GIs did the same. After my brother heard me, and saw my tears, he began to understand."

Frankie was not the only Gay to see active duty in Vietnam. A distant cousin, also named Marvin, was killed there in November of 1968. A real Marvin Gay had gone to war and died. The closest big star Marvin Gaye got to the battlefield was *playing* a soldier in a made-for-TV movie produced by future Beverly Hills 90210 impresario Aaron Spelling, not unlike the way he played a rock singer for Berry Gordy. He felt as hollow as when he'd been compelled to record the fake Tammi Terrell duets.

"He had this confused look on his face," Marvin's younger bother confirms. "He felt useless about the war in Vietnam. He said, 'Damn, Frankie, what can I do?' I let him know that he could fight in so many other ways, especially through his music. We were taught by my mother and father not to say things that produce bad images. But it was difficult for Marvin, because in his business bad images are a very saleable commodity. Our parents taught us a lot of love. There was no hate; you couldn't even say the word. And you do not ever hurt another person. So it's strange that Lucifer should come into our house and do what he did . . ." His voice trails off to a place no interviewer could possibly follow. It was Frankie who rushed to the family home that horrible April afternoon in 1984 to find his brother Marvin dead of multiple gunshot wounds and the weapon in the hands of their father. Frankie Gay is haunted by that day, and always will be. "Other people grieve and then get over it, get beyond it," he explains. "But every time I turn on the radio and hear Marvin's voice, the wound reopens and it all comes back."

In the song he'd been presented by Obie Benson and Al Cleveland, Marvin found a way to channel his sorrow for Tammi Terrell, his empathy for his brother's plight, and his own professional frustration into an artistic statement addressing the social and spiritual anguish he saw sweeping the real world, the one that existed outside Motown's candystripe walls. The shootings of Martin Luther King and Bobby Kennedy had hit him hard. The violence in the streets of Detroit in '67, the streets of Chicago during the Democratic National Convention in '68, and on a grassy knoll at Kent State University in 1970 seemed like eruptions of insanity. Seeing a man walk on the moon when there was unaddressed economic desperation within two miles of his own home was not at all inspirational; it was surreal and depressing. What the hell *was* going on?

The singer's expanding awareness had begun to strike terror in the hearts of his label's press liaisons. As part of the Motown finishing process, its stars were taught to offer nothing beyond bland, inoffensive pleasantry in interview. (This was so ingrained that all these years later it still afflicted more than a few people I spoke to for this book.) Despite his publicists' strict admonitions not to talk about anything controversial, Marvin would show up for interviews carrying well-thumbed copies of books by Malcolm X and Carlos Castaneda. As he told Jack Ryan, "In 1969 or 1970 I began to re-evaluate my whole concept of what I wanted my music to say. I was very much affected by letters my brother was sending me from Vietnam, as well as the social situation here at home. I realised that I had to put my own fantasies behind me if I wanted to write songs that would reach the souls of people. I wanted them to take a look at what was happening in the world."

"Take a look" is a key concept when discussing Marvin Gaye. The singer was hardly an activist in the traditional sense. A voyeur by nature, he wouldn't have been found at the love-in *or* on the picket line. What he knew he gleaned mostly from television or the newspapers or in conversation with the few who were allowed to penetrate his insular environment. When smoke from burning homes and businesses in Detroit's infamous 1967 "race riot" scented even the air in his tony neighborhood, Marvin was watching the action unfold on TV from the safety of his living room couch, no different from anybody else in America. What he did with this input, however, was very different from your garden-variety couch potato. The collision of these images of horror and injustice with the sense of righteousness that had been instilled in (or beaten into) him as a child produced an activism of the imagination that, when it found the proper musical context, would move untold millions of people. This new song that had fallen from heaven, through Obie Benson and into his life was just the creative jumpstart he needed.

After he'd worked with Benson and Cleveland to put his personal stamp on What's Going On, Marvin was so energised that he tracked down Berry Gordy to give him the good news personally. "I remember being in the Bahamas trying to relax and take a vacation," Gordy told a TV interviewer. "He called and said, 'Lookit, I've got to release this album. I've got these songs, it's great.' When he told me they were protest songs, I said, 'Marvin, why do you want to ruin your career? Why do you want to put out a song about the Vietnam War, police brutality and all of these things? You've got all these great love songs. You're the hottest artist, the sex symbol of the '60s and '70s . . .'"

Motown was a carefully choreographed black and tan Camelot. Outside its candystriped walls cultural revolution had been raging for years, but inside the Hitsville fortress the tried-and-true Motown Sound was still serenading blissfully unaware teens in the heart of a maltshop America that no longer existed. Some of the candystriping had been repainted paisley to keep up with what the kids were wearing, but the effect was the same. No-one knew better than Gaye how much Gordy disliked people coloring outside the boxes that had been desig-nated for them, so we must assume that the devilish *provocateur* in Marvin got precisely the reaction he was looking for.

As an indication of how far removed from the

streets – both literal and metaphoric – Berry Gordy now was, when rioting raged in the streets of Detroit in July 1967 he was in Las Vegas at the Flamingo Hotel with Diana Ross And The Supremes. He was horrified to hear that Dancing In The Street had become the themesong for the insurrection. Because so many corporate changes can be traced to this time period, it is tempting to portray Berry Gordy's romance with Southern California as part of the "white flight" out of urban Detroit that began in earnest before the ashes from the conflagration were even cool. Gordy's movements, however, were part of a personal choreography he'd been quietly orchestrating for years. As the folks back home were to find out, it wasn't so much that Mr Gordy had lost touch with the street. He was on a different road altogether.

To further disassociate himself from the tidy Motown box labeled Marvin Gaye, the singer drastically altered his appearance. Like John Lennon and Jim Morrison in the rock arena, Marvin grew a beard and dispensed with image-conscious fashion in favor of funkier, more casual attire. When people looked at Marvin Gaye, he wanted them to see someone they'd never seen before. And with his next single he was determined, despite Berry's reservations, to make damn sure that they heard something they'd never heard before.

Marvin and arranger David Van De Pitte worked to expand on the groove that he and Obie Benson had developed in the living room on Outer Drive. "As I began to get a handle on what he wanted," the arranger says, "my first thought was that it was never gonna fly, because this is not like anything else that's been done here before. I told Marvin I didn't think we were gonna get away with it. 'I don't care, man, I'm gonna do what I'm gonna do,' he said. After that we both got into a kind of 'the hell with the company' mode. Whatever happened, happened."

Marvin had his sights set on the unorthodox from the outset. Van De Pitte says that the singer didn't want to use Funk Brother drummers Uriel Jones or Pistol Allen for this project, that he wanted to stay away from anything resembling a standard Motown beat. The arranger brought in veteran big band drummer Chet Forest, who was augmented by a phalanx of percussionists: Jack Ashford on tambourine, Eddie Brown on bongos and congas, Earl Derouen on congas and Jack Brokensha on vibes and assorted percussive toys. "The atmosphere was pretty charged for a rhythm date," Ashford recalls. "We knew there was something different in the offing, really different." To complete the unusual feeling, the artist/producer was down in the Snakepit playing piano and leading the rhythm section himself. For his first self-produced single, Marvin Gaye was leaving nothing to chance.

Of course, as with the greatest and best-laid plans, two of the record's signature features happened almost entirely by chance. The lovely alto sax figure that opens the record, which Van De Pitte has heard at least eight musicians claim credit for, was the work of Eli Fontaine. Or, more accurately, his warm-up. When Fontaine had played enough to feel comfortable, he signaled that he was ready for a take. Marvin told him to go home; they already had what they needed. The confused saxophonist tried to explain that he had just been goofing around. "Well," Marvin replied, "you goof exquisitely. Thank you." The singer had been looking for a line that would expand on Fontaine's playing on the Baby I'm For Real intro. What he heard was so perfect that he knew he needed no retake, and decided not to spoil its perfection by having it reappear anywhere else in the song.

And the record's most imitated stylistic feature, Marvin's multi-layered lead vocal, was not part of the original blueprint. "That double lead voice was a mistake on my part," admits engineer Ken Sands. "Marvin had cut two lead vocals, and wanted me to prepare a tape with the rhythm track up the middle and each of his vocals on separate tracks so he could compare them. Once I played that two-track mix on a mono machine and he heard both voices at the same time by accident." This unintentional duet was not only kept, it became a creative strategy that was expanded and applied throughout the subsequent album and the rest of his career, becoming a hallmark of his vocal style.

Though the record would be a tour-de-force of Marvin's vocalising, the backgrounds were the work of amateurs, a gaggle of buddies that included two members of the Detroit Lions football team, Lem Barney and Mel Farr. Their parts weren't so much sung as chanted, and blended with the percussion-heavy track to create a tribal feel that was in part a nod to the long-haired, pot-puffing hippie tribe that the rebellious Gaye identified with (albeit from the safe distance of his Outer Drive retreat). In the break, these vocalists broke down into hip party chatter, while Gates (as Marvin was known to his friends, derived from Gayeskey, Harvey Fuqua's nickname for him) "sang" through the solo space that would normally have been filled by a saxophone. During the chatter in the fade there is a long, sustained intake of breath that sounds suspiciously like unlawful substances being ingested.

"They had a room off to the side of the studio that had originally been designed to give the horns separation," recalls Jack Ashford. "Jack Brokensha and I had our percussion stuff set up in there, but for some reason all the guys who smoked grass used to do it in there. There was so much smoke in there that you couldn't see across the room. Jack and I didn't smoke, but I know I got high just breathing the air. Marvin chain-smoked reefer, and he made no attempt to hide it. He floated around with a joint in his mouth, going from guy to guy checking the parts. He was everywhere; you could tell he was really excited. When we started playing this stuff it was really different, and I don't think it was just the air that I was breathing. There were things happening that other producers would never have even tried."

The record chugged along on a relaxed groove that in anybody else's hands might have degenerated into MOR, yet this would be the most avant-garde hit Motown had ever had. It begins with one of the most recognisable sax intros in all of pop, yet not only is the hook not repeated, the saxophone itself never reappears. The primal pulse of the chanting and percussion is countered by the refinement of David Van De Pitte's orchestration. The chatter of happy voices imparts a party-time flavor to a song that is deadly serious. The lyric expresses extreme hurt and anger, yet the song never gives in to either. His handling of the entreaty "Picket lines and picket signs/Don't punish me with brutality" is so rhythmically nuanced that the harshness of the images melts before the simple dignity of the request. His solution to the death and desperation that surrounded him – "War is not the answer/For only love can conquer hate" – sounded hopelessly naive to disillusioned hippies left holding bouquets of dead flowers in the aftermath of the massacre that took place at Kent State University only two weeks before Gaye commenced this recording. What Marvin offered was not *naïveté* – he'd wept at the taking of Martin Luther King and Malcolm X as well as for the Kennedys and Kent State – but a faith through which all could be reconciled. What's Going On was a record in which absolutely nothing could have worked, but everything did. For once the singer's conflicts and contradictions worked to his musical advantage.

It took multiple mixes to nail it down, but Marvin was ecstatic. He'd succeeded in creating something that was unlike anything else spit out by the Motown machine. Perhaps as important, What's Going On was as different from I Heard It Through The Grapevine as Whitfield's record had been from run-of-the-mill Motown three years earlier. The musicians knew it too. Most of the time, the session players didn't have the slightest idea what a song was called or the artist for whom it was intended These supremely gifted musicians

– veterans who'd played head arrangements with the likes of Charlie Parker, Dizzy Gillespie, Sonny Stitt and Yusef Lateef – often looked down their noses at the pop music they were hired to roll out on the Gordy assembly line. Not on June 1, 1970. When bassist James Jamerson got home from work that night, he told his wife he had just cut a classic.

Imagine Marvin's reaction, then, when Berry Gordy refused to release What's Going On, reportedly calling it "the worst thing I've ever heard in my life".

6 Stubborn Kinda Fella

I was sitting around incensed, mad and angry.
When I get that way I don't do anything. That's my
only weapon.

Marvin Gaye

MARVIN IMMEDIATELY ISSUED AN ULTIMATUM
of his own: until Berry Gordy and his Quality Control
cabal came to their senses and released What's Going On,
the singer would record nothing more for the company.

It was almost as if Motown had anticipated this
rocky road ahead. They rushed the compilation *Super Hits*
into the marketplace in September 1970 with a cover that
portrayed Marvin as a cartoon superhero. This rendering
acknowledged his elevation in status with Grapevine and

the Terrell duets, but how could Marvin Gaye hope to be a superman if they wouldn't let him spread his wings and fly?

Clay McMurray understands Gaye's frustration. The young producer had been brought into the company by Norman Whitfield after his novelty version of Stand By Me by Spyder Turner had become an unlikely hit in early '67 on MGM Records. (It probably didn't hurt that two of Turner's vocal impressions on the record were of Smokey Robinson and David Ruffin.) Like Whitfield, McMurray served his apprenticeship as a Quality Control assistant. But he was having his own problems with the department at around the same time it rejected What's Going On.

"With all due respect to the talents of the people in Quality Control," McMurray says, "it was all based on a concept that was adhered to because it had been successful in the past. Politically and creatively, a lot of songs were squashed because they didn't fit. You have to watch out, though, that the concept doesn't become so predictable it gets stale. I had the same problem with If I Was Your Woman by Gladys Knight. I got fought tooth and nail, because the concept of the day had been set when Norman cut Grapevine on her, and that uptempo thing was all they wanted. I pointed out that her greatest successes before she got to Motown were with ballads like Letter Full Of Tears. I stood my ground and got the record out, but it was a battle."

Considering how often I heard McMurray's sentiments echoed – as Johnny Bristol pointed out, the truly creative are always going to have a gripe about *something* – and for all the stories of battles fought to put new ideas and different sounds into play at Hitsville, most of the conflicts were resolved at the top of the charts. The label's catalog is deep in wonderful music, but little was commercially wasted. On balance, very few hits fell through the cracks at Motown. If some records didn't get as far as they should have, in those glory years the label's own success might have been the greatest hindrance. There were only so many records the company could work and the charts would accommodate at any given time, even for the almighty Motown.

Having acknowledged that, however, we must also consider that the three most important Marvin Gaye records to this point – Grapevine, Baby I'm For Real and now What's Going On – had all been turned down by Quality Control, and three times the company's hand had to be forced to get them released. Pure coincidence? Not likely. It leads one to more probable conclusion that greater forces than the department were at work here. At

Motown, there was only one force greater than Quality Control.

Marvin's relationship with Berry Gordy followed his usual path of peaks and valleys. He had no trouble exploiting his proximity to the throne when it suited his purposes, but he also didn't hesitate to butt heads with his powerful brother-in-law. Scarred by a contentious and physically abusive upbringing, Marvin followed the classic pattern of seeking out, and then rebelling against, authority figures. After escaping Reverend Gay's fundamentalist house of horrors by enlisting in the Air Force (an encounter with authority that was every bit the disaster you'd imagine), it had been Harvey Fuqua and was now Berry Gordy Jr, who would become his ultimate professional authority figure and therefore his nemesis.

In one of Hank Cosby's first memories of Marvin Gaye, the young singer was in a fistfight with Berry Gordy. The pair were going at it out on the front lawn of Hitsville right there on West Grand Boulevard. "It was raining and they were slipping all over the place," recalls Cosby with a chuckle. "It was actually funny, more comical than anything. Marvin was real skinny, a 90-pound weakling, but he was a mouthy guy. Berry's attitude with the young people was 'I made you a star. I've done everything for you.

I'm taking you there, so you be quiet and listen to *me*.' But Marvin wouldn't take orders from anybody.'"

This fight was the perfect metaphor for their relationship. Gordy, a former professional boxer, could have taken stringbean Gaye apart without breathing hard. Gaye, for his part, was probably convinced he could take the boss. Mr Gordy, meanwhile, regarded his headstrong star with a mixture of affection and annoyance. Both were intensified when Gaye became a member of the Gordy family. "To be honest with you," Cosby says, "Marvin and Berry were not on good terms much of the time. And after Marvin married his sister, it seemed like they stayed on bad terms."

Elaine Jesmer: "From what Marvin told me, it was not a good situation between them. Mostly because he wouldn't kowtow. And of course Berry had the Berry image to maintain, so Marvin was always gonna fight him. There was some very personal aspect to this. It was one of those things between men that women don't get. A guy thing, where it was like they had their dicks in their hands and were having some kind of pissing contest. Marvin was not the sort to ever give up, so you just knew it was gonna be a war of wills forever."

Marvin's relationship with Anna Gordy Gaye was even more combustible. Road manager Joe Schaffner spent a lot of time around the couple. "In the beginning there was a lot of love," he says. "Anna was supportive, but always very jealous too. Being older, she was experienced enough to know how it was out on the road. There were always a lot of ladies around, and these girls knew when you were coming to town. If they happened to be married, they'd be planning to have a good time that night. These girls hounded Marvin. They'd spend a fortune on clothes, but the tags would still be on 'em. I'm serious! They'd wear these clothes to impress, then return them the next day. Oh, Anna knew all about *those* kind of women.

"Marvin loved the attention, but he got accused of doing a lot of things he never did. Basically he didn't do anything on the road. He had plenty of lust in his heart, but he didn't act on it. In those days a pornographic magazine would keep him happy after a show. In all the years I was out with him, there was one time – and *only* one time – that he slipped. It was in Chicago, and he discovered that he'd caught the clap. We were flying home and he was so scared about what was gonna happen. Then I got an idea. I told the stewardess that we required a wheelchair when we landed in Detroit. I wheeled him off the plane in the chair, and had a doctor friend of Marvin's meet us at the house. Our cover story was that he was suffering from exhaustion and pneumonia, which the good doctor confirmed. It worked until his real condition had been treated. Being burned like that, he learned his lesson.

"He loved his wife. They'd talk on the phone for hours almost every night. Course, this was also Anna's way of checking up on him. If you get off work at six o'clock, your wife expects you home within the next hour. If it goes too long beyond that, she knows something else is happening, and her own mind becomes her worst enemy at that point. They'd argue about that whenever he came off the road, even if they'd talked every night. One time they had an argument sitting in the car parked in front of a police station. She got so mad she whacked him across the head with her high-heeled shoe, and there was blood trickling down his face. Jealousy starts a whole ugly chain. Because he loved her, he was capable of great jealousy too. He was convinced *she* was messing around, which she very well may have been. They started to provoke each other to do these crazy things."

Elgie Stover: "Marvin got mad at Anna one time when they lived on Appeline Street, and threw all her most expensive clothes out the window. You would've been a rich man if you'd parked a truck under *that* window. He threw Anna out of the house, and then the chinchillas and minks started flying. Anna's mother drove over in an El Dorado and picked up all this stuff; Mrs Gordy told her never to go back to Marvin. There were so many furs on the lawn that it looked like a damn mink farm."

In January of 1970 Anna Gordy Gaye had flown to Los Angeles for an extended stay with her brother Berry. Marvin came out for a few weeks too, but it was a sign of the how far their marriage had deteriorated that he stayed in separate accommodations at the top of Mulholland Drive and seldom saw his wife. They fought whenever he did, mostly about his refusal to get with the company program and cut their hits and get out there on the road to support them. Baby, I'm For Real (the romantic song they'd written together for the Originals) was at Number 1 on the R&B charts and its Gaye-Stover-Gaye follow-up, The Bells, was about to be released, but the emotional harmony that had produced those lovesongs seemed very far away now. So he simply avoided Anna, taking in the local sights and buying the luxury trinkets that Grapevine and Baby I'm For Real made available to him. He fell in love with a blue Excalibur (with wolf carpeting, no less) that comedienne Phyllis Diller had put on the market. He paid the asking price with no haggling and had the car shipped back to Detroit.

As comfortable as he was on Outer Drive, it became more difficult for Marvin to shake the feeling that he was wearing Berry Gordy's hand-me-downs. This came bubbling to the surface when the Internal Revenue Service, which had not failed to note the monies that had been flowing to the singer through the Grapevine pipeline, came after him in the first of what would be an ongoing series of ugly tax disputes.

Kenneth Stover had followed his brother Elgie from Cleveland, and became a driver and aide to Mother Gordy while Elgie sometimes worked in a similar capacity for Pops. The brothers, plus Joe Schaffner when he wasn't on a road assignment with another Motown artist, acted as support team for the reclusive Gaye. It was Kenny who witnessed the first IRS strike. "I came home from work one day," he remembers, "and Marvin was in the living room with some white guy. Things seemed to get a little agitated, and as Marvin was walking him to the door he started cursing the guy out. It got very loud, and I heard Marvin yell 'Fuck you!' as he slammed the door on him. I went to see what was happening, and Marvin was *mad* – 'Those motherfuckers . . .' Then we heard some noise outside and ran back to the door. The dude had cranked up the Fleetwood that was parked in the drive-way and pulled off with it. The IRS had taken his car.

"Of course, they didn't know there was a Rolls-Royce and an Excalibur parked in the garage. He didn't take them out after that for fear they'd be snatched too. He got a jeep to drive around in; he didn't really care about those luxury cars anyway. He used to say, 'Kenny, man, I could live in a one-room shack and drive the raggediest car. Don't mean nothin' to me, man.' He wanted to show 'em that they couldn't take any of the things from him that *really* counted."

Joe Schaffner: "Money didn't mean anything to him. It was just another tool. If he had it, he spent it. If somebody was in need, he'd try and do something for them. He helped people out, and most of the time it stayed between him and the other person. He wouldn't want anybody else to know. He was especially good to his family; he gave them whatever they wanted.. And when Tammi began to get sick, he'd buy things for her. Little surprises to keep her spirits up. There was nothing he hoped to gain by this – he was just trying to make her feel better."

He was apparently an equally soft touch when it came to people he didn't even know. "This guy came to the door one time," says Elgie Stover. "Never seen him before, had no idea how he found the house. He starts in with some crazy, made-up story about how he needed all this money. The story was so unconvincing that my mind can't even recall the details. And Marvin was gonna give it to him! He was writing out a check to this guy, when Anna happened on the scene and put a quick stop to it. She couldn't believe that Marvin was falling for this guy's line, to the tune of $1200. That was quite a pile of cash in those days."

The taxman could turn off the royalty tap, and attach whatever else they could find. They were unable to touch the house on Outer Drive, because Berry Gordy had given it to Anna. (Joe Schaffner contends that the house actually belonged to neither, and was registered to Jobete Music for tax purposes. Berry Gordy was considerably smarter that his brother-in-law when it came to the taxman.) Likewise, the only safe vehicle was the one Berry had given to his sister. And so Marvin Gaye, an international star and a proud man, found himself essentially living off the charity of his brother-in-law.

Elgie Stover: "The IRS closed him down for awhile there. He was broke, didn't have *any* money. Marvin went through a major depression. This dispute was settled after a while, though they'd come back at him again even stronger in Los Angeles. Later people would always ask him when he was gonna do another *What's Going On*, and he'd say 'when I get that depressed'. See, Anna was a Gordy, so she could afford to go off to California for six months and leave him there. She was married to Marvin, but she was still part of a rich family. He couldn't hold her back. If he didn't do for her, she could always go to Berry. So Marvin never had control of his wife, because she could always do what she wanted to. In fact, she owned him. That was not always a bad thing. She kept him under control. I remember one night at the Twenty Grand club she went on-stage and hit him because he was making eyes at some girl. Marched right up on that stage and socked him! But she believed in Marvin absolutely as an artist, and she was a smart businesswoman who was good for his career."

Elgie's brother Kenneth Stover remembers that the eruptions at this time had more to do with finance than romance: "I guess there was always going to be friction because Marvin was a rebellious person, and Anna was used to getting her way. Both of them stood in there strong. There was not as much arguing as I'm told there had been before. The static he was getting from Anna at that time was about how he was handling his money problems. But he was also coming into a creative time, and Anna stood behind him all the way."

(Indeed, had Marvin Gaye not had the motivating and politically advantageous presence of Anna Gordy behind him, it is conceivable that his story might have wound up not so very different from another of Motown's extravagantly talented but tragically temperamental artists, David Ruffin.)

Once Anna heard What's Going On she was passionately back in her husband's corner. Despite her influence with Berry, however, she couldn't overcome the thumbs-down of the Quality Control department and reverse her brother's decision not to release the single. The rejection was final. But if Berry Gordy thought by shelving the record that Marvin's artistic fit of temper would pass and he would settle back down to the business of making acceptable hits, he was wrong. And if he thought that Marvin's empty bank account and attached assets would help pressure him into returning to the straight and narrow, he was wrong again.

"Marvin said something to me once that I will never, *ever* forget," Elgie Stover says, measuring each word. "It still makes me strong just to think about it. He used to let me wear his clothes and jewelry and drive his cars, so I always looked good when I went out with the boys. One day I asked him why he had no interest in these things. 'I don't need any of that stuff,' he told me, 'because *I* am a jewel.' Do you hear what this man was saying? He enjoyed having the money, but he always said that he could live without it and be just as happy as a bum. Even as a bum he'd still be a jewel."

Hard-headed as a diamond, Marvin would wait them out. He'd heard protesters advising that the only way for an individual to fight the war machine was not to allow his body to be used as an instrument of that war, and this was the way he approached his battle with Motown. He understood that his only means of fighting the company machine was to refuse to let himself be used as one of its cogs. The passive resistance preached by Martin Luther King was the only path. He was already a part-time live performer at best, now he would simply cease recording altogether until What's Going On was released.

Meanwhile, the jewel would shine in a different setting. Marvin Gaye had decided to become a professional football player for the hometown Detroit Lions. That he had never played the game before didn't appear to bother him. Though he bragged to a newspaper reporter in 1963 that in high school he'd starred on the football, baseball, track and swimming teams, he was now more forthcoming with Jack Saylor of the Detroit Free Press: "My father wanted me in church most of the time. I played very little sandlot football and I got me a few whippin's for staying after school watching the team practice." Yet the singer insisted, "I have confidence I could play."

His hubris blithely ignored not only his utter lack of experience, but that at age 31 he was already well past professional prime, and that he basically *was* the 90-pound weakling of Hank Cosby's earlier description. In his own mind, he had made football players recording stars – or would, if Motown ever released the damn record. How difficult could it be to make a recording star a football player? This was evidence of Marvin's unshakable belief in himself, and of his distance from anything remotely resembling reality.

Richard Morris: "I ran into Marvin one day and he asked if I played football. He said he was on his way to play with some of the Detroit Lions and suggested I come along. I said, 'No thanks Marvin, those guys are *professional* football players. You aren't getting me anywhere near there.' We laughed a bit, and he went off. Next day he came up hurting from being out there with those guys. He caught an interception, and I guess Lem Barney had told him not to try running it back. But Marvin being Marvin, he couldn't resist, and they busted him up."

Still, by the time the Lions were readying themselves for pre-season workouts, he actually looked like the athlete he'd always wanted to be. "He was running around with the football players," Hank Cosby remembers, "they showed him how to work his body and what to do. He changed from a skinny little guy to this 200-pound monster. When I first met him, his wife used to beat him up. I swear to God! She used to run him out of the house and actually physically beat on him. But when he bulked up, he slapped her one time and had no more trouble with her. He always had the attitude, but now he could back it up."

Despite this impressive physical transformation, Obie Benson still laughs at the thought of Marvin in the blue and silver uniform of the Detroit Lions: "I told him that the girls screaming and hollering for him when he sang were the wives of the players, and that the guys on the field would be waiting for him. They been playing football all their lives, and you just start and think you're gonna waltz on to the field and make the team? They gonna kill you, man!"

They never got the chance. Nobody in the Lions' management wanted to risk the repercussions of injuring a national treasure, so the joking offer of a tryout that coach Joe Schmidt had made during a post-game celebration the previous season was nixed by the higher-ups.

Marvin didn't take the news well. He pouted and claimed, more than a little disingenuously, that he'd canceled a half-million dollars in live bookings to follow his dream of athletic excellence. (He had been declining most performance offers long before the football fantasy appeared.) And he continued to insist, despite any evidence to support him, that on the field he could have been a contender.

This unfounded belief that he could compete if he set his mind to it was typical. It was the same with golf, which had become a Motown craze in the first flush of the label's success. Berry Gordy took it up, then Smokey Robinson and a host of others. "Whatever Berry did, everybody else did," Jack Ashford snorts in disgust. "If he went to take a shit a three o'clock the whole company would shut down. They walked like him, talked like him. It was awful, so transparent. He played chess; soon everybody else did. When he started playing golf, they all went out and bought clubs."

Golf – an almost exclusively a white upper-middle-class leisure activity until Tiger Woods emerged in the 1990s – became the sport of choice among successful Motown artists and executives. Marvin was part of the company crowd that met at the Palmer Park course but, true to form, he put his own spin on the golfball. He soon found a way to make this genteel sport dangerous, though he was the one who almost always suffered the brunt of the consequences.

"Marvin couldn't play golf worth a shit," Elgie Stover states bluntly. "He bought the best equipment, and wore the best clothes, but he couldn't play at all. Guys who'd never played before could beat him, but that didn't stop him. He thought he had his own technique. He tried to psych people out, put pressure on 'em by making big bets on crucial shots. But the more he bet, the better they got. Marvin bought several Cadillac El Dorados when they first came out, and all the hustlers over at the golf course used to fight among themselves to see who was gonna get first crack at all them fine cars. These guys were hustling him; that's what they did for a living. They didn't have jobs, and didn't need 'em as long as Marvin was around to be hustled." In those freewheeling days before the IRS came calling, Marvin would sometimes lose between $10,000 and $20,000 dollars in an afternoon to slippery characters with names like Mississippi Junior ("uh, just make the check out to 'cash'"). Didn't matter – Marvin always thought he had a system working for him, and there was no telling him otherwise.

Unbeknown to Marvin, he had an ally at the company in his silent war over What's Going On. At first glance, Harry Balk would seem an unlikely champion for such a progressive record. Balk was an industry veteran long before he arrived at Motown. He'd managed Little Willie John, and had guided the careers of such Michigan rock stalwarts as Del Shannon and Johnny And The Hurricanes. Balk's most recent success had been Oh How Happy by the Shades Of Blue on his own Impact label when Motown hired him to helm Rare Earth Records, the company's attempt to penetrate the white rock market. Balk was soon overseeing much of Motown's creative department, as Ralph Seltzer and his team of mostly white administrators spent more time administrating in the absence of Berry Gordy. Though it was never publicly acknowledged, Berry Gordy had been a committed California resident as early as 1967. By mid '70 he probably spent more time in Vegas than he did in Detroit.

"As records were finished I'd get acetates coming across my desk on their way to being evaluated by the Quality Control department," Harry Balk explains. "One day this Marvin Gaye acetate was sent to me by mistake, mixed in with some white product. I just fell on the floor when I heard it. I *loved* it, and made a tape of it before sending the acetate on. I listened to it over and over, and fell more in love with it. I started playing it for people who came into my office. Of course everybody will tell you now how wonderful they thought What's Going On was, but I played it for the hot producers – Norman Whitfield, Hank Cosby, Frank Wilson – and got nothing but negative opinions. The only one that was really knocked out with it, *the only one*, was Stevie Wonder."

Ralph Terrana, who worked under Balk, confirms the missionary zeal of his boss: "He called me into his office and said he wanted my opinion on a record. To be honest, it didn't hit me. He looked at me and said, '*That* is a Number 1 record.' I made a joke about that's why they paid him the big bucks, but Harry really did sell Motown on What's Going On. Berry Gordy used to pitch his early songs to Harry Balk for Little Willie John; that's how far back those two go. Harry represents what the old record guys used to be. They were creative gamblers. They put out records on hunches, and if they had a gut feeling they went for it."

Despite their lengthy history, Balk's pitch to Berry Gordy was no more successful than Anna Gordy's had been. "Berry called me and said we needed to get Marvin Gaye product out. I told him I couldn't get Marvin into the studio. He wanted to be a football player, a boxer, a lumberjack – anything but a singer. When I brought up What's Going On, he didn't want to know. 'Ah, that Dizzy

Gillespie stuff in the middle, that scatting, it's old.' I told him it wasn't old, that the way Marvin had put it together was new. Nobody wanted to know. Quality Control turned it down. They were used to the 'baby baby' stuff, and this was a little hard for them to grasp."

When, months later, the company relented and finally released the single, it speaks volumes about where Motown was at that What's Going On was issued without Gordy's knowledge.

In the end, it was Marvin's stubbornness that carried the day. "We needed a Marvin Gaye record desperately," admits Executive Vice-President Barney Ales. "He made sure that's the one that was released, because it was the only one we had. Marvin, as people have probably told you, wasn't about to kowtow to anybody. Finally I had a talk with Billie Jean Brown and her Quality Control staff, and we agreed to put it out. Though Berry had pretty much moved to California at the time, the scheduling and releasing was done out of my office in Detroit. We just forwarded acetates to the coast for Berry – who was then, I believe, in the early stages of the Lady Sings The Blues movie – to listen to. So he didn't even know that What's Going On had been released."

Marvin had another surprise up his sleeve. In the final mix, just as the record was about to fade out, he grabbed the fader and pushed the track back up for a couple of seconds before it ebbed away for good. "It wasn't planned," says Steve Smith, the engineer on the session. "It was something that just happened. It was Marvin's mind trip, his way of saying 'fuck you' to the company, and I think more so to Berry Gordy. You think this song you hate is over? Surprise!" Obie Benson agrees. "It was a head trip," he chuckles, "a little fuck you from Marvin. Fuck you, with love. 'Because I *do* love you,' he'd say, 'in spite of yourself.'" (As Gordy had used the same device several years earlier on an "obnoxious" Contours record he knew certain people would hate, there may also have been an inside joke at work here.)

Barney Ales happened to be flying to Los Angeles on the January day in 1971 when What's Going On was finally released, and he knew he'd have some explaining to do at the other end. "You could occasionally roll the dice without Berry's permission at that time, but you had to have a hell of a reason. Berry went crazy when he found out we'd released What's Going On. He didn't like the record *at all*. Luckily, by the time my flight touched down in LA we already had reorders for 100,000 copies. And this was only the first day, mind you. When he found out we'd sold 100,000 in one day, his attitude changed."

As those figures demonstrate, What's Going On

The smooth-shaven, sharp-dressing young company man, an image
Marvin Gaye would seek to obliterate with *What's Going On*

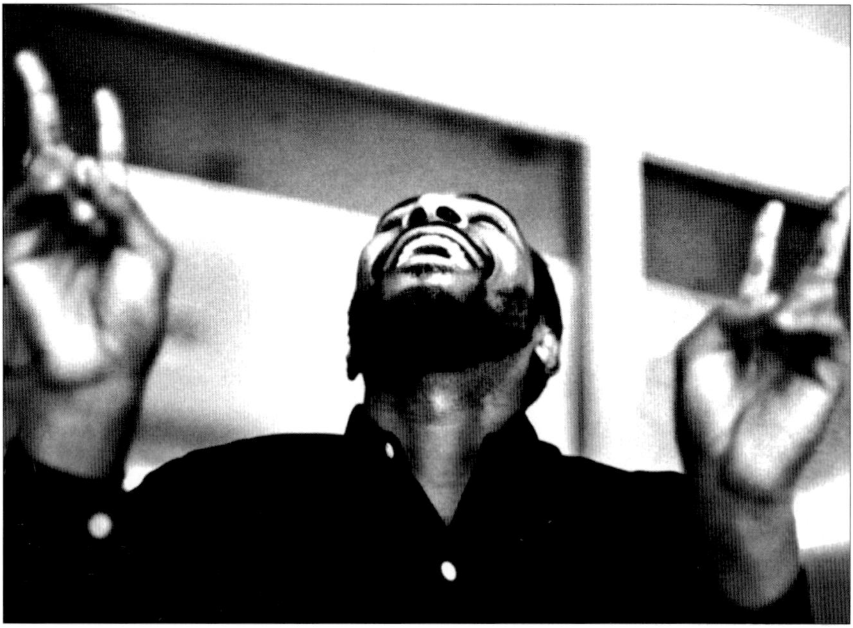

Jim Hendin

Among the many moods of Marvin Gaye
(these and all subsequent pictures come from the *What's Going On* photo shoot in March 1971)

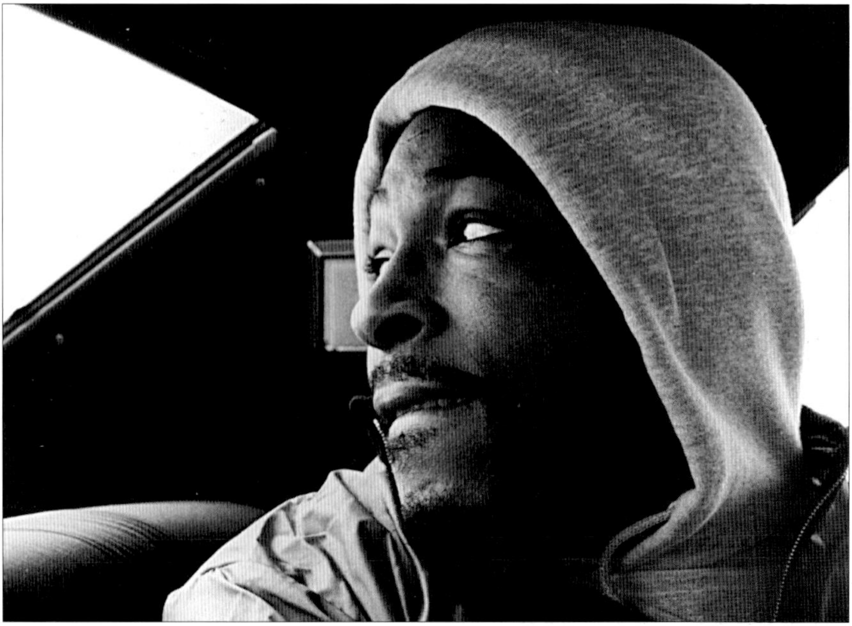

Jim Hendin

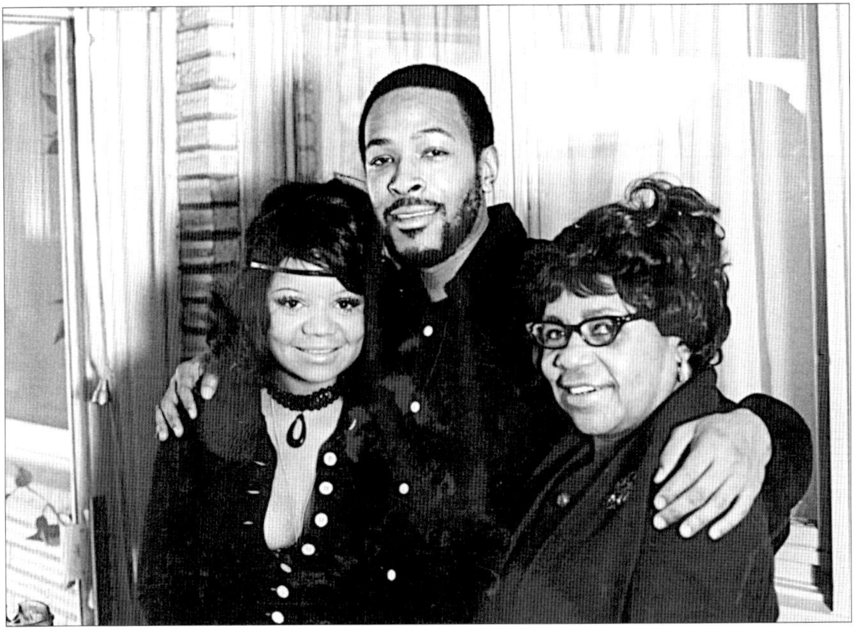

Jim Hendin

Marvin and his girls: wife Anna Gordy Gaye (left) and mother-in-law Bertha Gordy

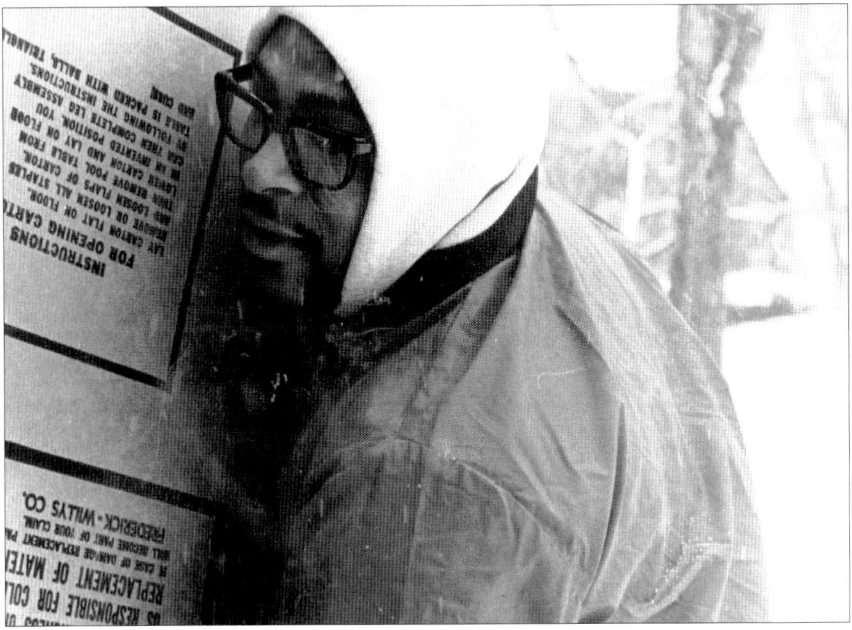

Jim Hendin

Marvin, the Motown mover

"Talk to me, so you can see . . ."

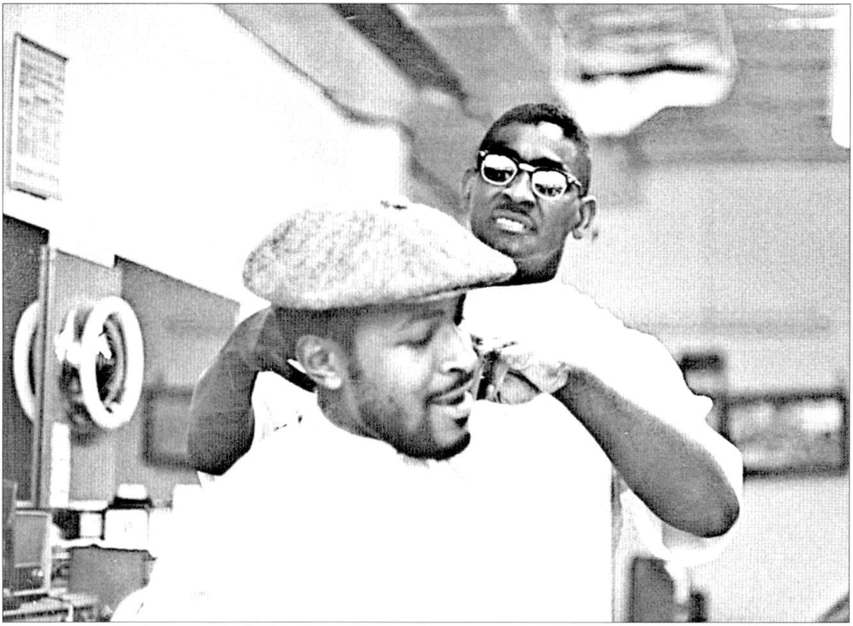

Jim Hendin

Ever the iconoclast, Marvin demonstrates his daring "hats-on" haircut technique

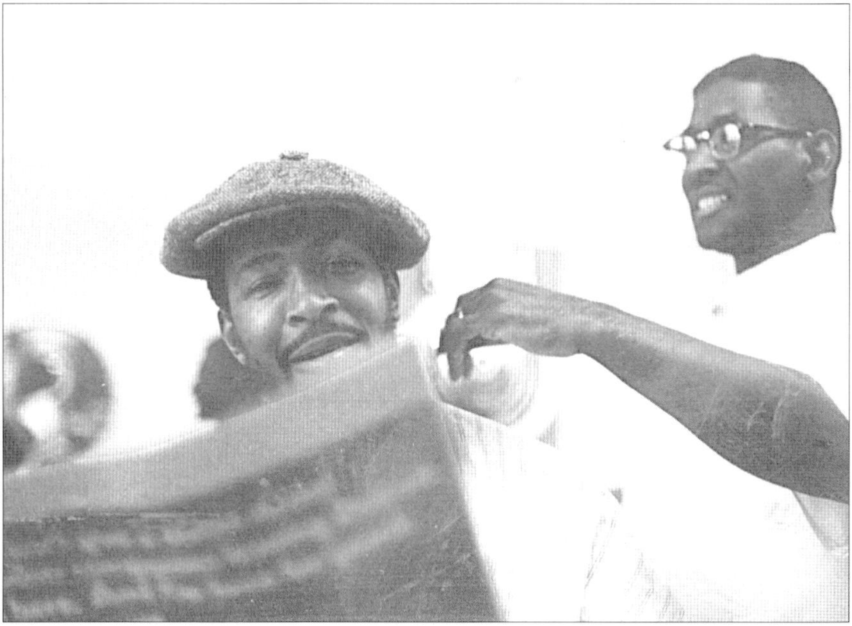

Jim Hendin

"I want everybody, as long as I'm here, to say,
'I wonder what Marvin is going to do'"

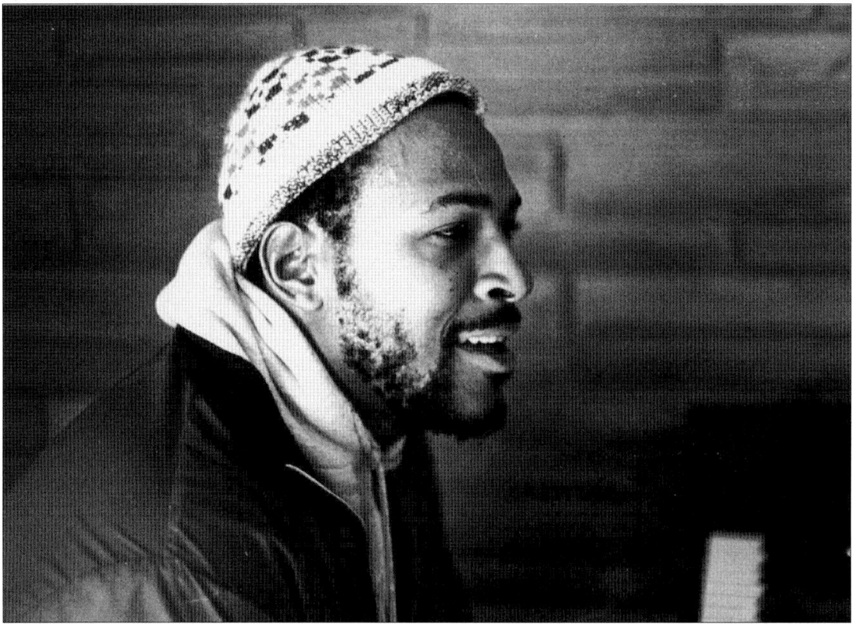

Jim Hendin

Dressed for action. Marvin would often make his creative colleagues take intense athletic breaks from their songwriting labors. "Oh man, don't remind me," groans Obie Benson

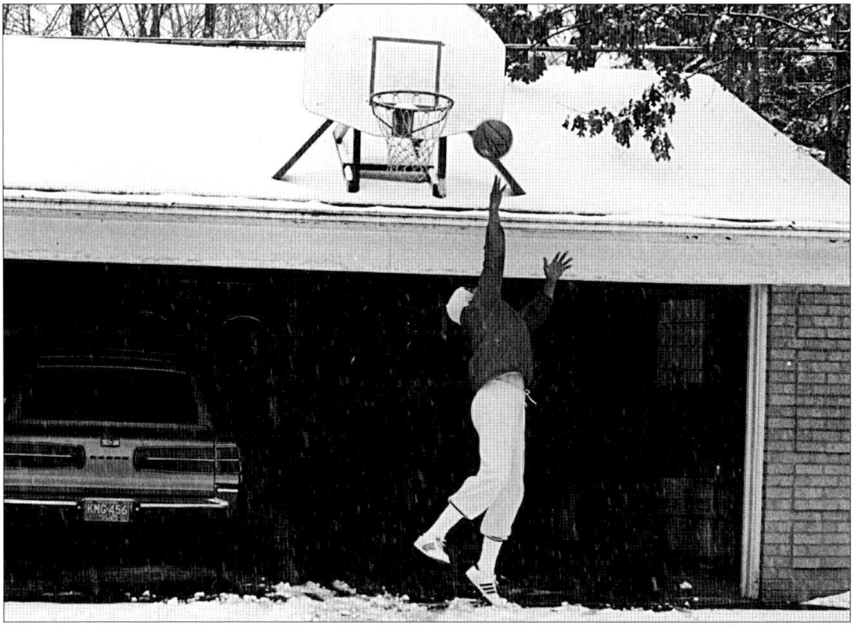

Jim Hendin

"When would the war stop? That's what I wanted to know . . . the war inside my soul"

was an immediate sensation, rocketing to Number 2 on the pop charts and Number 3 at R&B. (Curiously, neither the single nor the album that followed made any impression on the UK charts, one of the few times the UK has failed to embrace a progressive musical vision.) Motown had the hottest single in America ... and nothing to back it up with. The company's attitude immediately changed from "this is shit" to "give us an album's worth of this shit, *and quickly*".

Marvin had proven his point with the single so, given his contrary nature, he was in no hurry to crank out an album's worth of miracles at the company's bidding. Of course, he needed the revenue such an album would bring even more than Motown, but Marvin was never one to let necessity or logic temper the sweet exercise of refusal. "He loved to be asked to do things," Joe Schaffner recalls, "and he loved to say no. If somebody like Bob Hope called and said he'd like Marvin to appear on his TV show, it was a thrill for him to say no. He wanted you to call back; if you asked again that meant you really wanted him to do it. But on the first call he would always say no. It was the only way he felt in control."

He had always been difficult to get into the studio, and this didn't change just because he was now producing himself. But with Marvin the recalcitrant artist holding sway over Marvin the producer, it fell to arranger Van De Pitte to try and crack the whip.

David Van De Pitte: "Elgie Stover would call and tell me Marvin wanted a seven o'clock meeting. So I'd go over there and sit and wait, while he was out playing basketball or upstairs in bed meditating or whatever – anything but working on this album. I'm looking at my watch, because I've got 20 other people at the company waiting for me to deal with their stuff. I'd sit there for hours on end, waiting for the cat to show up. Many times he didn't show at all. Sometimes he'd call me back into his bedroom, and act surprised that I was there, and I'd have to remind him that we were supposedly making an album. He'd tell Elgie to get me some 30 – they were drinking Ballantine 30-year-old scotch at the time – and he'd be out in a minute. Then maybe he'd straggle out 45 minutes later.

"Finally it got to the point where I went downtown and basically threw in the towel. I said, 'Look, kids, I don't have time in my life for this. Nice man, wonderful music, but it's just not coming together. Somebody's gotta get behind him with a big stick, and that's not my job.' So I told Harry Balk that maybe he'd better get me off this project, because it wasn't going anywhere."

Balk commiserated with his disgruntled arranger, and smoothed his ruffled feathers with a $2500 bonus as a sort of "combat pay". But Balk hints at another dimension to Van De Pitte's frustration. "David was mad," Harry remembers. "He was saying 'This guy is hitting little piano notes and he expects me to make something of it. I'm a trained musician, not some musical secretary, and I don't need this,' and so forth. David happened to be an excellent arranger, and it was sometimes difficult for trained musicians of his caliber to deal with the company's raw, unschooled talent."

Marvin's recalcitrance likely had less to do with laziness than with calculation. What Marvin may have been asking for, once again in his passive-aggressive way, was a "pretty-please" from the company, and more specifically from the man who'd turned the record down in the first place. So one evening late in February a limo pulled up to the Outer Drive house, and Berry Gordy, on one of his visits to Detroit from "the Coast," decamped for a pow-wow. He explained to a bemused Marvin that he was losing $100,000 a day by not having a new album in the marketplace. The typical Motown strategy would've been to throw together an unconnected assortment of tracks from the vaults under the title of the hit single, but Gordy knew enough not to threaten this particular contrary artist.

*

Aware that Gaye had committed to a film acting job in Los Angeles at the beginning of April, he made the singer a proposition: he could cut the album of his dreams – in fact, Gordy would block off time over at Studio B for the artist's exclusive use, a luxury unheard-of down at the factory – but only if he finished by the time he was due in LA. And, according to Elgie Stover, the wily Gordy sealed the deal by offering to place a friendly little wager. Whether it was based on the delivery schedule or commercial performance is not known, but the amount was substantial enough for Stover to claim that inveterate gambler Gaye had "bet his life" on this album. The limo driver was called in to draw up and witness the arrangement, and Berry Gordy was off into the night.

The clock was running. Marvin Gaye had 30 days in which to make his miracle.

7 Come Together

I work best under pressure and when I'm depres-
sed. The world's never been as depressing as it
is right now. We're poisoning the planet, killing
our young men in the streets and going to war
around the world. Human rights, that's the
theme.

Marvin Gaye

THOUGH MARVIN CLAIMED TO HAVE THE
entire album written when Van De Pitte first met with
him on the single, all he really had to express his strong
emotions was a vague concept and a few song fragments
scattered around his living room floor. The material came
together piecemeal in the months when he refused to

record, and some songs were not completed until after the recording process had commenced.

As a composer, Gaye was hardly what you'd call a formal constructionist in the Duke Ellington mold. He was more like Bob Dylan, who'd assemble the elements, set the general parameters, and then cut loose to see where it would lead. Dylan didn't plan his famous "wild mercury music", but he knew it when he heard it. So it was with Marvin. He understood the emotional and spiritual thrust of what he wanted to express, but exactly how that was to be transmitted through word and music was a mystery the album would be a process of working out. Over the years he'd acknowledge musical precedents for the suite that resulted, among them the ghetto tone poems of Duke Ellington, the use of sweet strings over funk grooves pioneered by Isaac Hayes, and the gospel hymns he'd heard and sung as a child. And, closer to his present home, the continuity of sound that marked the Four Tops album *Still Waters*. But just as nothing could have predicted the confluence of elements that produced the single, so it would be with the album.

Regarding the accepted story of his recording "strike", the truth is that he did a fair amount of studio work during this time. Much of it was tinkering with the tracks from the arrangements of standards he'd commissioned from jazz pianist and composer Bobby Scott in 1967, which he would not feel vocally capable of tackling until much later in the '70s, and would not be released as the album *Vulnerable* until 1997. In addition, there is recorded evidence to suggest he was also working on early versions of three of the four songs that would comprise side two of *Let's Get It On*, his 1973 follow-up to *What's Going On*. But he kept his vow in that he delivered no new material to the company. What he recorded was for himself.

During that time, however, he had developed two other songs with Obie Benson and Al Cleveland, Save The Children and Wholy Holy. Of the latter, Benson says "I had in my head a very up-tempo reggae kind of thing. Marvin broke it all down, and then rebuilt it as a spiritual, a jazz classic. What he brought to it blew my mind." Including the title track, the three Benson-Gaye-Cleveland songs would comprise the heart of the *What's Going On* album. According to the Four Tops, there were other songs they were working on, but these were scrapped when he and Marvin had a falling out over song credits. Apparently Gaye wanted to add the names of friends to the songs if they'd given him a word he liked, to which Benson and Cleveland objected strenuously. The estrangement didn't last long, but it did preclude the inclusion of other material by the trio.

Even with the success of the 45, there was still plenty of skepticism about the album around the office. "I got teased all the time," reports Elgie Stover, a key collaborator. "When I'd leave Motown to go over to Marvin's house, they'd all say, 'yea, you go over there and write them national anthems with Marvin.' That was the way Norman Whitfield put it. They had *no idea* what we were up to."

Marvin liked it that way. He also went out of his way to assemble his team from the neglected corners of the Motown closet. According to Hank Cosby, "Marvin liked to get losers – I shouldn't say 'losers'; maybe underdogs is a better term. He saw potential in these people that others didn't, and would take time with them and try to put 'em together and push 'em up. That was one of the wonderful things about Marvin; that was the real Marvin Gaye."

One such beneficiary was James Nyx. To most of the employees at Hitsville, Mr Nyx was the elderly, impeccably-dressed gentleman who ran the elevator in the company's Woodward Avenue building, and little more. "He'd hand out his lyrics to anyone who showed the slightest interest," remembers Johnny Bristol. "He was completely tone deaf, but that wouldn't stop him from singing them to you. He was a very nice man, but nobody took him seriously. Nobody but Marvin. He took the time to discover that Mr Nyx was an excellent writer of words." Marvin heard the poetry, and unlocked the melodies that turned the words into song, and for his effort was rewarded with what would become the album's most powerful track.

"Marvin had a good tune, sort of blues-like, but he didn't have any words for it," Nyx told Neely Tucker of the Detroit Free Press. "We started putting some stuff in there about how rough things were around town. We laughed about putting some stuff in there about high taxes, 'cos both of us owed a lot. And we talked about how the government would send guys to the moon, but not help folks in the ghetto. But we still didn't have a name. Then I was home reading the paper one morning, and saw a headline that said something about the 'inner city' of Detroit. And I said, 'Damn, that's it.'" It certainly was, and that's how the track that early tape boxes referred to as The Tail End – because it was the last track cut – became Inner City Blues.

The album's most basic "message" piece Save The Children had an interesting genesis. "The song was an extension of the What's Going On concept," Obie Benson explains. "If you can't love anybody else, at least love the children. Give them a world for their future. As we were working on it, we could hear the kids playing around the house, or see them through the windows playing around the swingset in the back yard. We realised that the instinct to protect your offspring is the bottom line of everything, so we wanted to make people look at the current situation in that light. Al Cleveland, Marvin and I, each of us wrote a complete version of the song, and then we took the best parts from each. Man, I wish you could hear the original, when we couldn't figure out which lyrics to choose. It was damn near 'bout an hour long."

The subject of children was one that hit literally close to home. The childlike Marvin Gaye had always responded to the openness and vulnerability of the little ones. Millie Gill of the Velvelettes remembers unexpectedly having to bring her baby to the studio one day and, while the other men recoiled in terror, Marvin gladly volunteered for diaper duty. "The kids were always on his mind," says Kenneth Stover. "He spent a lot of time with Little Marvin and the others. This was when he was getting a lot of pressure from every direction – the tax people, the company people. He really enjoyed his time with the kids because they didn't want nothing but to be with him. He'd spend hours in Little Marvin's bedroom, just playing guitar and singing to him and the others. He couldn't play much, maybe a couple of chords, and he made up stuff as he went along. Some were just nonsense songs to make them laugh. But then he'd work it around to what was really on his mind. It was like he was saying the things a father should say to his kids, but he was saying it through music."

For Marvin at this time the process of composition included spontaneous auditioning rituals. His collaborators might find themselves suddenly yanked out of songwriting class for an enforced recess in which they had to engage him in a game of all-out basketball, or try to keep up with him on an extended run in the early winter snow. Still buff from his Lions experience, only his football buddies and Elgie Stover could keep up with him. For the softer creative types, it was a torment to be endured.

"Oh man, don't remind me," Obie Benson groans, though he thinks he understands the motivation for these daily drills. "If you've noticed, Marvin spent a lot of time trying to get away from music. He lived the stuff he wrote, it was all about *him*. Even the songs he didn't write had to express something he could relate to himself. Writing was very real to him; it wasn't abstract. He could see things other people couldn't see. That's a blessing, but there's a price too. He would spend hours and hours writing, pulling these feelings up out of himself. But then he'd have to get away from it. Basketball, football, boxing, all that shit. And oh yes, the jogging. I'd say 'Man, you're killing me with this shit,' and he'd laugh. I complained, but I did it, and it's actually helped me later in life. That's just the way he went at everything. He didn't make decisions quick, but when he did, watch out! That boy could *apply himself*."

(It wasn't all boot camp at the Gaye compound. There was a joint ready by Marvin's piano at all times, and the liquor flowed for his friends who were so inclined. Elgie Stover even remembers a couple of "regulars" who were conspicuous by their absence whenever the 30-year-old scotch would run out. "I could drink a bit in those days too," Obie Benson admits in a way that let me know he was not nearly so discriminating. "I would be just throwin' em down. Marvin didn't drink too much, and he'd ask me what I was trying to do. I'd say, 'I'm trying to outdrink this motherfucker in the mirror!' He'd just shake his head." Marvin didn't drink to be sociable; he was strictly a professional drinker. He didn't really like alcohol, but he found that a few nips helped soften the edges of the performance anxiety that gripped him in the studio as well as on the stage.)

*

With Marvin, songwriting was seldom a bolt out of the blue. It was more like a slow stew, where he'd fiddle with the ingredients and let it simmer until he was satisfied. And just because a song had been recorded and mixed didn't mean that it was finished. Consider the convoluted path of God Is Love. It was first cut by the Monitors in several sessions that spanned the first half of 1968. It was much slower than the version we would come to know from *What's Going On*, and nowhere was the title mentioned in the song. In fact, the lyrics are revealed to be an earlier and altogether different version of his classic Just To Keep You Satisfied, a change subsequent tapeboxes reflected. The completed record languished in the vaults for over two years until Marvin appropriated the track and added his own lead vocal, with entirely new words that changed the song to God Is Love, exquisitely completing the version that was released as the B-side of the What's Going On single. This ballad treatment is one of the jewels of the Marvin Gaye catalog, to the extent that it makes one wonder why he then re-recorded it as the jaunty fragment (only 1:42) that it becomes in the album tapestry.

The Just To Keep You Satisfied lyric, meanwhile, had a new musical bed crafted that was cut on the same tracking date as What's Going On. This version was sung by the Originals. Though completed, it too clocked a couple of years on the shelf until Marvin once again took it back (though he'd keep some of the Originals' backing vocals) and wrote a new set of words for the version he used to close the 1973 album *Let's Get It On*. Or consider Sad Tomorrows, a late '69 track cut with the Originals in mind but completed by Marvin's own vocal a year later and eventually released as the B-side of the Mercy Mercy Me single in July '71. At the same time, however, the Sad Tomorrows lyrics become, virtually without change, the words to the *What's Going On* song Flyin' High (In The Friendly Sky) – but with an almost completely different writing credit!

Once the songs were roughly sketched, the tracking sessions took place on March 17, 19 and 20. According to Johnny Griffith, Marvin ran an easygoing ship: "He was probably the most relaxed person that I ever worked with at Motown, and the most considerate. The rhythm dates started at 11 in the morning, and you know musicians – everybody straggled in with very little sleep, because a good many of our guys would put in a full day in the Snakepit and then go out and blow all night in the clubs. So during our first break, Marvin would say, 'C'mon back here, I've got some food,' and there'd be fried chicken, mashed potatoes, all the trimmings. It was just what the guys needed, and it made the session social, more like a party. And if we went overtime, nobody complained because it was an enjoyable experience.

"Of course," Griffith adds, "the musicians also *really* enjoyed playing this music. 'Now this is something a little different': Marvin said that over and over. He'd go over to each musician and go, 'This goes something like this,' and he'd sing something to give them some idea of a direction. It was important that Marvin was down there playing piano himself. He didn't know exactly what he wanted, but as we'd play it developed. He'd be constantly tinkering with things. The arranger could sketch things out, but Marvin would have to hear it before he'd really know if it fit. The arranger was usually right by the producer's side, and whatever was written on paper would change through trial and error." Though he was not quite a Funk Brother, Marvin's early Motown apprenticeship as a drummer gave him a special link to the musicians that only Stevie Wonder, whom the Brotherhood had tutored, could match.

According to percussionist Jack Brokensha, "The big difference was that Marvin was one of the few guys who were *capable* of producing his own session. Usually we'd be working with people who couldn't even count the band off. That's where the famous Snakepit count-off came from: 'a one, a two, you know what to do' – *boom*. Whereas Marvin and Smokey, and Stevie Wonder when he got a little older, had a developed musical vision of what was wanted."

With this new music he was trying to capture, it wasn't that he was asking these seasoned musicians to play jazz. What this music appealed to was the jazz musician's natural love of adventure.

Uriel Jones: "We felt closer to Marvin than a lot of the other producers. Most producers came in and just wanted to buy what we'd done for them in the past, which wasn't much of a challenge. But Marvin would always come in with something a little different in mind. You never knew what you were going to get with Marvin, and that's why we looked forward to sessions with him. This time, he was so deep into what he was doing that we got deeper into it too. He had his own idea of what he wanted, and we had to work at it – working the Motown *out* of it, so to speak."

Some past accounts have suggested that James Jamerson's playing on these sessions showed evidence of his personal deterioration, a contention that Jack Ashford vigorously disputes. "No, no, no, *no*," the percussionist fairly shouts. "I don't think I can name a single date where

James was so drunk or high that he couldn't perform. Now, I'm not stupid, and I can't make any claims for him outside the studio. But when it came to the music, he was rock-steady with that. I understand that his playing did deteriorate out in California, but in Detroit during this time? No. *No!* JJ was thundering, man, he was *thundering."*

James Green confirms this. "Jamerson was on top of his game," says the engineer who recorded the first tracking session. "I can't think of a better bassist in the world. I got to sit there and watch this guy reinvent the way the bass was played every day. I've listened to jazz all my life, listening to guys play chords, whole notes, but here was a guy fingering a bass like you'd finger a guitar. Not just attempting it, but doing it, and doing it with such ease. He'd be the first one to look at the chart, play a few notes, get it down. Then he'd already be into variations on the part while the others were still figuring out the basic chart. Not only could he play it, he understood what it was trying to say."

The question of which of the two listed bassists, Jamerson and Bob Babbitt, played on which tracks has been the subject of much speculation. Now, largely thanks to the research of Harry Weinger, we have a clear answer. We know James played on the single, recorded well before the album. Jamerson also played the first tracking day for the LP, March 17 in the Snakepit. Cut sequentially was the suite of songs that would follow the single on side one. Side two was cut on the next tracking date, March 19, over in Studio B with Babbitt on bass, and also in sequence. Marvin had been unhappy with the version of Mercy Mercy Me he'd cut in Studio A, because he began this second session by recutting it. So it's Jamerson on the first five songs and Babbitt on the final four. David Van De Pitte remembers the two bassists playing together on Inner City Blues, an exciting proposition. Babbitt, however, says that both parts are his; that Marvin called him back in on March 20 to overdub the second bass line.

The album's deep and varied use of percussion was a strikingly original signature. The band Santana was already well-known for the use of conga and timbales in their rock'n'roll attack, but Marvin's deployment contained only a passing Latin inflection. His percussion phalanx – Eddie Brown on bongos and congas, Earl DeRouen on conga, Jack Brokensha on vibes, bells and a variety of other items, and Jack Ashford on tambourine and anything else he could get his hands on – was more urban, like the multi-layered sound of the city as you'd hear it through an open window in a part of town the good times have passed over. Kit drummer Chet Forest just kept the beat solid, and let the others do their dance around him. And if all this percussion wasn't enough, somewhere in the mix is the sound of Marvin hitting a cardboard box with a drumstick.

Jack Ashford: "On Mercy Mercy Me I tried out this block I'd just gotten. It was wooden and shaped like a tube. It was concave, with a middle section that had a hole, 'bout one inch in diameter, running all the way through it. I've got very big hands, so when I cupped it and hit it, you got that very unusual *pow pow pow* sound you hear on that record. It came out that way because my hand was acting like an echo chamber. That gave it such a sound! Marvin had been looking for some different textures, and when he first heard it he screamed, *'That's it!'* I can't tell you how many people I've talked to over the years who've begged me to tell 'em how I got that sound. Because you'll never hear a sound like it on any other record. That block was unique; somebody stole it from me, so that was the one and only time I got to use it."

Among the general concepts Marvin had thrown at his arranger was that the album had to flow from beginning to end. Van De Pitte suggested having segue music linking the tracks, but the solution they arrived at was more interesting still. "The studio technology was still pretty primitive," Steve Smith explains: "To edit, you had to physically cut the tape with a blade. So when the basic rhythm tracks were done, Ken Sands and Cal Harris took the multi-tracks and edited the entire album together by hand. It was quite an accomplishment." Normally horn, string and vocal overdubs are applied one song at a time. With the basic tracks already cut into the larger collage, the overdubs were then applied to the entire album, adding immeasurably to the cohesiveness and flow of the finished product.

Getting a grip on the charts was problematic at first. "Marvin would play me a couple of notes on the piano and want me to write it for the vibes," says Van De Pitte. "I'd have to tell him that those notes weren't even *on* the vibes, that it was an improper register for that instrument; celeste or bells maybe. Marvin was hearing something in his head, but I'd have to tell him that bagpipes – or whatever – couldn't get the sound he was looking for. We'd have these little arguments. Good-natured *musical* arguments, though they'd occasionally get heated."

The clash between trained musicians who know the rules and musical primitives asking the impossible is as old as the rules themselves. Marvin described his side to Ben Fong-Torres in 1972: "There has to be another dimension. Why are there cracks in the keys on the piano, for instance? There's some music in those cracks. Why couldn't there be another musical system in fact, a whole new system that I could invent. And why is it that when something is out of tune, it's not music? It's still a note. Can get a little complex, you know, but that's the area, the unknown area, that I want to get into. I'd like a bunch of those sour notes to make into a symphony." (Marvin Gaye, say hello to Charles Ives.)

The only lingering sour note in Van De Pitte's relationship with Gaye was Marvin's statement in that same Rolling Stone interview that he "conceived every bit of the music" on *What's Going On*, an assertion that still rankles the arranger, and rightly so. It was pure nonsense; Gaye had help, and inspired help at that, every step of the way. Marvin's Achilles heel creatively was he that was a supremely collaborative artist whose ego would never let him fully exploit this strength. Marvin's comment bespoke his feeling of insecurity in the face of Van De Pitte's musical education, and personal issues of control that he'd wrestled with all his life.

According to Ken Sands, who engineered some of the overdub sessions, "Marvin relied on David to translate the feel he wanted. That was pretty much the standard producer/arranger relationship in those days. He'd lie there on the couch in front of the board and yell things out: 'I like that. I don't like that. Take that four bars out of letter A.' The producers went for feel, and had the arrangers to tend to the smaller details. The arrangers were there to steer the ship. They were at the tiller, and the captain would say, 'Let's take a course ten degrees to the left.'"

Many producers acknowledged the role of their arrangers. "I always wrote my own charts, even though I didn't have any formal training," says Deke Richards, whose Motown zenith was the work he did as the organizing member of the production collective known as the Corporation. "In the beginning I used David Van De Pitte as a tool, because he could write so much faster than I could. I'd tell him that I wanted this here, and that there, and he'd know exactly what I was talking about. From there though, he'd say, 'well, that's great. But let me do this, and then let's try to do this . . .'. That's where I gained an immense respect for David. He turned out to be more than a tool; he made my work better. That's what arrangers are supposed to do, and he did."

It is the view of Larry Nozero, a saxophonist who played Van De Pitte's charts on this and many other dates, that the arranger outdid himself here: "I think Marvin gave Dave a green light to be even more creative than he'd normally be on a Motown session. So David was a large influence on the way the album turned out musically. The orchestrations he wrote were stepping out from the norm Motown expected of their arrangers. So you had Marvin Gaye stepping out, and encouraging Van De Pitte to go along with him."

The end result here was that, as occasionally happens when the instructed and the instinctive collide, they made each other's work better. This was actually, Johnny Griffith explains, a Motown tradition: "It was the beginning of a new era in disguise. For a long time Motown was not looked upon as a serious situation [by the musicians]. It was something we'd do to pick up a little extra cash. The music was written by people who were not really songwriters. They wrote their own way, with very unorthodox ways of doing things. They'd come in with ideas that were not strange to them, but to a trained musician there are things you do and things you don't do. But they'd just do whatever they wanted to do! You had to really pay attention. You'd go off and be playing wrong, but to them it was right. That turned out to be a really valuable experience for me, because I was forced to think in ways I hadn't been trained to."

Marvin's moondreams may have been exasperating for Dave Van De Pitte to try and pin down, but the effort produced horn and string charts of extraordinary lushness and color. The string players, on loan from the Detroit Symphony, were the first to get an idea of what the finished music would sound like. They were stunned by the picture their own instruments completed during the marathon March 26 session in which orchestration was added to the entire album. "This music caught most of them off-guard," reports Johnny Griffith, who was there to overdub some celeste. "Motown sessions were a gas to these [Symphony] people. They'd come in at midnight after their gig and have fun playing this pop music. But as soon as they saw David's charts they knew they were on to something special, and the juxtaposition of their parts against the tracks blew them away. You could see it on their faces as they played."

You could see it in Marvin's face as well. "That was the night Dave Van De Pitte really shined," agrees Bob Ohlsson, who then worked the Studio B nightshift. "The strings really completed the character of the whole thing. Dave was out in the studio conducting. Marvin came into the booth and sat down. Halfway through the first run-through, I saw that his eyes were a little moist. Soon the tears were streaming down. I think that was the first moment that he understood how well Van De Pitte had captured the musical thoughts in his head, and that this album was really going to be everything he'd wanted it to be. It completely blew his mind. It was an unforget-table session."

On this charmed project, Marvin was even getting karmic breaks from the studio. "B was a difficult room sound-wise," Ohlsson explains. "We had been experimenting with how to better capture strings. I'd been working with a fellow named Sam Ross, who'd been hired away from Curtis Mayfield's operation in Chicago. He had excellent ideas, and we completely reshaped the sound of the room with panels and partitions. Marvin was in the right place at the right time to take advantage of all the experimen-tation we'd been doing."

With Van De Pitte's ripe orchestrations on top and the percussion-heavy rhythm tracks that Elgie Stover says they called "black bottoms", you already had something special cooking on both ends. Mix in the many vocal moods of Marvin Gaye, and you had distinctive elements on all levels that blended into a musically unique and sonically accomplished whole.

"I felt like I'd finally learned to sing," Marvin explained to David Ritz. "I'd been studying the micro-phone for a dozen years, and I suddenly saw what I'd been doing wrong. I'd been singing too loud. One night I was listening to a record by Lester Young, the horn player, and it came to me. Relax, just relax. It's all going to be all right." Without realising it, in the relaxed conviction of his singing on this album he would achieve his longtime ambition to become a black Sinatra; not by mimicking Ol' Blue Eyes as he'd done in the past, but by letting his own vocal self come forth.

The multiple voices they'd stumbled on to for the single became a full-blown style woven throughout the album. On the 45 of What's Going On the effect is employed tentatively; the multiple Marvins sounding simply like ghosts of the lead vocal. On the album the relationships between the many layers of vocals, and the way they lay in the atmospheric musical bed have become the very point of the record. His mastery of multiple voicings began early. At Moonglows rehearsals under the demanding Harvey Fuqua, Marvin made a habit of learning *every* group member's part. If you listen to his counterpoint on the duets with Tammi Terrell and his work with the Originals, you'll hear many of the rudiments of the multi-layer style. Many say Marvin was at his best when singing with a partner, and with *What's Going On* it proved as true when he was his own partner: Marvin and Marvin.

"He had three voices," Berry Gordy told Harvey Kubernik in 1994, "Marvin on top of Marvin on top of

Marvin. Just incredible. The truest artist I've ever known. Whatever he was going through in his life he put on the records. So if you want to know Marvin, just listen to one of his records."

Joe Schaffner: "Those voices were often like a conversation. He would sing the song a certain way, but the backgrounds he'd sing a different way, making it like an answer. When we talk we say what we've already thought in our minds that we want to express. But at the same time we have other voices in the back of our minds where we might think, 'No, I'm not gonna say *that*.' So Marvin's backgrounds would often say what he was really thinking, while his lead was what his mind wanted his mouth to say."

Because the themes of this album – war, peace, ecology, politics, economics, salvation – were light years removed from the rock 'n' romance box Motown had assigned him, he took a whole new approach to recording his vocals. "We kept all the love attraction out of it," Elgie Stover says. "There was no talk of women and men anywhere on that album. I'll put it this way: before recording those vocals Marvin used to go in his room and lay down and masturbate for hours, just to keep that energy out of his mind and his performance." A novel twist, no doubt, on the old prizefight wisdom that has a boxer refraining from sex before a big fight. (Of course, with Marvin there was always the simpler possibility that he just *really* enjoyed practicing the safest sex of all.)

Marvin no longer had to be coaxed into the studio, but he did like to ease into a session, especially the vocal dates where it was just him, the engineer and a couple of friends. Marvin the producer was even more relaxed with Marvin the singer than he'd been with the musicians. "Marvin used to like to sit around in the control room and talk for a while," says Russ Terrana, who is not challenged when he claims to have mixed 89 number one records in a career that included twenty years with Motown. "It was his way of loosening up. My impression is that he didn't prepare for vocal sessions very much; he preferred to come in cold and catch it spontaneously. We might sit around talking for a couple of hours – about philosophy, theology, sports, whatever. Then he might be in the middle of a sentence when he'd suddenly stop and say, 'I've got an idea,' and head out into the studio. He knew when it was ready to happen for him. Before then he wouldn't push it, and you couldn't push him."

His ideas frequently included last-minute lyric inspirations as well as approaches to vocal technique. "He was still messing with the words right up to the recording," Steve Smith claims. "Some things he didn't come up with until he was singing them. There was a lot of that in the song What's Happening Brother, including the line 'Will our ballclub win the pennant, do you think they have a chance' – that was right off the top of his head. In his mind nothing was ever really finished. He'd always have one more idea he wanted to try out."

Messing with the written word was something Marvin was already known for, albeit in a lighthearted vein. "Marvin always amazed us," says Sylvia Moy of earlier sessions when he was in the hands of other producers. "When you'd give him the melody and the lyrics, he'd just take off on you – changing all the lyrics, improvising something totally nuts, totally *crazy*. He'd have us all in stitches. It was his way of keeping things loose. He liked it loose and easygoing." It was also indicative of a creative impulse that never rested, and was finally let off the leash for these recordings.

Engineer Ken Sands describes the atmosphere at the vocal sessions that took place from March 27 through March 30: "The control room would be dark, and we'd darken the studio, just keeping a single light on Marvin. The smell of incense would be in the air, as well as the smell of other substances. We gave Marvin a hand-held microphone so he would have freedom of movement. He'd always have two or three friends sitting on the black couch in front of the console, giving him encouragement and feedback. We'd do take after take, and then innumerable playbacks as he'd pick out pieces to keep."

Obie Benson: "I had come back in off a Four Tops tour, and I was in the studio when he recorded the vocals on my songs. He asked me to bring my guitar, and had me play along from the control room. This was not recorded; it was only for him to sing to along with the track. There was something about the way I played that seemed to bring him back to the feeling he had when we were working on the songs in his living room. He'd taught me some different voicings on the guitar, so it was like his own voice playing along with him, understand? He'd say, 'Ob, it's important to have the technical movements connect, but it's more important to get that feeling you have in your head.' I wasn't a very good guitarist, really, but I had a feel of my own that Marvin liked. My old man taught it to me a long time ago. I play with my fingers, and it has to do with how you use the fingernails. It was kinda like slap bass, except on the guitar. My uncle used to play the blues that way; that cat had *long* fingernails, man."

The smell of "other substances" emanating from the singer's sessions had become notorious. Marvin was convinced that marijuana was soon to be legalised, and he and his buddies would sit around trying to come up with potential pot adverts. "Try the Marvin Redeye brand, friends and neighbors. No seeds, no sticks, no stems. Just clean smooth smoke. Hear that guy laughing? He just sampled Marvin Redeye's private blend," was the way Elgie Stover recollected one "script". Marvin Redeye had no great interest in commerce, but this was one commercial endorsement he wanted to sew up well ahead of time.

Among his partners in this recreational crime was engineer Steve Smith, then the youngest Motown employee: "Nobody could tell Marvin what to do, but they could certainly tell *me*. They called me up one day and said that under no circumstances was there to be any smoking of pot in the studio. I relayed this to Marvin and he just laughed. 'Oh really?,' he said. 'Okay, I won't smoke any more pot. From now on I'll just smoke weed.'" (There had recently been an extremely short-lived Motown subsidiary label called Weed Records, whose slogan proclaimed, "All your favorite artists are on Weed.")

"The next night Motown's head of security just *happened* to come by the studio when we were cutting vocals. All of us who smoked were a little afraid of John Corsi. Not Marvin. He just happened to be rolling a joint, as he so often did during those sessions, and when he saw Corsi he casually finished rolling it up, lit it and took a big hit. He said (mimicking a voice holding smoke in), 'Hey

John, how ya doing? Good to see you; I didn't realise you were a fan.' Then he exhaled these huge clouds of sweet smoke. He did it just to fuck with Corsi, the authority figure. The Rebel King, that's what I used to call Marvin. But he did it with great humor."

There was certainly some humor (at least in retrospect) when, during a visit to Outer Drive by the regal couple Esther Gordy Edwards and husband Michigan State Representative George Edwards, little Marvin brought out daddy's stash box to play with. But being a prominent member of the Motown family did offer certain advantages in this area, says Elgie Stover: "At that time Motown was so big in Detroit, didn't nobody bother the artists. One time the police stopped me when I was driving Marvin's car and the ashtray was full of roaches. Man, you'd get 20 years for that in Detroit then! So I told 'em it wasn't my car, and the officer said, 'We know. It belongs to Marvin Pentz Gaye.' Just the way he leaned on *Pentz*, a middle name that almost nobody knew, was to let me know that they knew exactly what was going on. They let it slide.

"Marvin didn't care. He'd fire up a joint in front of his *mama*. We used to have so much fun when his mama came to visit; maybe because the father always stayed home in DC. She was a better entertainer than Marvin.

She'd smell the weed when we'd be in his room smoking, and she'd yell, 'Somebody in there cookin' them pots?' Before she went home she asked me for some seeds, and the next time we came through Washington she had her own little garden happening out back for us."

(Russ Terrana remembers an incident a few years later when Marvin, despite his vow never to sing with another partner, was somehow coaxed or flattered into recording a lackluster album of duets with Diana Ross: "The first time we went in to cut vocals with the two singers, Berry Gordy was there, and the whole entourage. It was a real zoo. Well, as you've probably heard, Marvin liked to smoke a joint when he sang. So he's out in the studio happily puffing away, and Diana comes into the control room in a huff. 'I'm pregnant and I can't be out there while he's smoking that marijuana and bla bla bla.' Marvin is sitting out in the studio in a chair, cool as can be, taking a hit now and then. So Berry gets on the talkback – the room suddenly very quiet – and says, 'Uh, Marvin, Diana's pregnant and she doesn't want you to be smoking a joint.' Marvin stopped for a second, looked up and said, 'Then I can't sing.' For the rest of the album they'd come in separately. There was not a single moment when they actually sang together." Marvin may have been the Rebel

King, but he could also be King Prick when the mood struck.)

Though he'd been forced to give up his fantasy of becoming a Detroit Lion, the singer had not surrendered his athletic delusions completely. Steve Smith recalls Marvin showing up for sessions looking like he'd been mugged, the result of his newfound interest in boxing. Gaye was managing a local fighter, but couldn't resist stepping into the ring himself. "This guy put a real whipping on Marvin one day," Smith says. "His face was *so* swollen. But he didn't seem to mind." No, to the child who was never allowed to play sports and the young man who never went to war, it probably mattered less that he'd been whipped than that he took his whipping like a man.

Coming down the stretch on the 30-day deadline, there were a thousand loose ends to tie up. Ed Wolfrum remembers Marvin even coming over to United Sound when things got jammed up at Studio B, and paying for these supplemental sessions out of his own pocket. But there was also room for one last major stroke of musical inspiration. Once again it involved Marvin rummaging around the dustiest corners of the Motown closet and finding a neglected jewel. Marvin dropped by a club one night and was taken with the tenor saxophone stylings of one William "Wild Bill" Moore. Wild Bill was a Texas native who'd come up hard with southwestern "territory" big bands of the 1940s, subsequently recording sides for a number of R&B labels such as Aladdin, Modern and Starday-King, though he quickly faded back into the life of horn for hire. Moore had played the occasional Motown session over the years, but by then was not too highly regarded around town.

Jack Ashford: "He was an older guy, Lester Young vintage. When they dissed him as an old man, they didn't know what the hell they were talking about. Bill Moore could play. See how Marvin was? He could *hear*. Because this cat could *blow*, man, he could bring some fire."

Johnny Griffith had known the saxophonist for years. "Wild Bill was a unique person," he says with obvious affection. "I worked with him when I was in high school. I was the youngest one in the band, and Bill had been out there for – oh God, we used to tease him – what seemed like a hundred years. When I was coming up, they called what he did a 'beer garden' style of saxophone playing. He'd gladly walk the bar if that's what it took to get over. He'd go all around the room playing, and if you were talking he'd get right up in your face and growl with his horn. He had that old-style growling thing in his playing. At one time I guess he'd been more prominent, but then the style changed on him. What was valued among the session players at the company was smoother jazz chops. But Bill was a beautiful guy, and kept a good frame of mind despite this. He always had a big smile on his face."

Just as Marvin had tapped into the musicians' love of jazz to pull inspired basic tracks out of them, he saw in this anachronistic rhythm and blues honker the perfect spice for his divinely inspired stew. He took Bill Moore into the studio late one night and after sharing the sacramental joint ("So this is what the stars smoke," said Wild Bill approvingly), turned him loose to splatter tenor sax all over his tracks like an R&B Rauschenberg. Wild Bill improvised across the entire stitched-together canvas of the album, and then Marvin went back and kept the bits that caught his fancy, weaving Moore's distinctive sound in and out like another voice. It added absolute magic to Mercy Mercy Me. Marvin's plea for ecological awareness sails along on a smooth groove until Wild Bill's tenor comes raging in, sounding like a wounded member of some endangered species, adding weight to the music and urgency to the message. Few solos have said so much with so little.

"I'll never forget when Marvin sent this saxophone player to see me," says Hank Cosby, who was then in charge of contracting session musicians. "Wild Bill Moore comes in and says, 'Hank, Marvin said you would give me $500 for playing a solo on his record.' I said *what???* This was one of Marvin's pot-smoking buddies; that's what made me mad at first. Brother, what you been smoking? I could hire *10* musicians for that. So of course Marvin comes screaming on the phone, even though he knew I couldn't authorise it. Marvin sometimes liked to create little problems just to keep the pot stirred. He knew didn't nobody get no $500 for playing a solo . . ." What Hank didn't realise was that the solo had lasted for almost the entire album. In the end Wild Bill probably got his $500, though how much of it might've come directly out of Marvin's pocket is unknown.

But it wasn't all down to divine inspiration and good ganja. There was plenty of old-fashioned elbow grease, and some of the smaller adjustments were the most difficult to get right. To do the female voices he called upon Louvain Demps, Marlene Barrow and Jackie Hicks. Called the Andantes, these singers dwelt even deeper in the shadows of Motown than the Originals. In their capacity as the female house backing vocalists, the Andantes appeared on more Motown records than any other group. They'd worked with Marvin as far back as Mr Sandman in '61. (Demps had in fact been the very first client of the Rayber Music Company, Berry and second wife Raynoma Gordy's 1958 venture that evolved into Tamla-Motown.) Yet, unlike the Originals, in all those years the Andantes never had a record of their own. Their only scheduled release, Like A Nightmare, was withdrawn before it could even reach the streets in 1964. Officially, the Andantes never existed.

What Gaye envisioned was not your typical vocal group stuff; the trio were there to add a female texture that was not always easy for Marvin to articulate. "We all loved him so much, but he was extremely, *extremely* hard to work with on this project," admits Louvain Demps. "It was like he had all this knowledge; in his head and in his heart he could hear everything. But we couldn't always hear exactly where he was trying to go. He had us doing a lot of little things just for texture, and that could be difficult to understand. They were frustrating sessions for us. He would sing it to us over and over again until we got it exactly as he was hearing it. He was quite picky. Most of the time the Andantes could sing whatever you wanted with no difficulty, but he was hard to please on this album. He was not the usual Marvin, at least as we knew him. His mood was not as jovial. Usually he kidded a lot and was always laughing. Not this time. His mood was more serious. I got the impression that he felt like he was fighting for his life, that his life was somehow riding on this album, so every last detail had to be perfect. That can be hard to live up to."

Marvin was responding to the demands of his perfectionism, but was also reacting to the rapidly approaching deadline. Not only was the wager with Berry Gordy hanging over his head, but he had the film commitment to honor. Having failed to demonstrate any measure of acting ability in the TV movie The Ballad Of Andy Crocker (starring Lee Majors, the Six Million Dollar Man), Marvin had somehow landed a supporting role in an equally unpromising big-screen biker quickie called Chrome & Hot Leather. When the album kicked into gear and he tried to back out, the film producers made litigious noises. He was locked into a flight to Los Angeles in early April. The album would simply have to be completed by then.

Marvin the producer was now feeling all the pressure that Marvin the artist never had to contend with, and the frazzle was beginning to show. Hank Cosby remembers that Marvin could be emotionally volatile under the best of circumstances. "He was the kind of guy that you'd see in the afternoon and everything was great," says the one-time sax player who met Gaye when both were backing Smokey Robinson And The Miracles on the road.

"But when you saw him that night he'd be down. Up, down, up, but never in between. If you catch him when he's up, he's the greatest guy in the world. But you catch him when he's down – look out."

Coming down the stretch both moods intensified. "Elgie Stover went through all of it with Marvin," says Steve Smith. "He took a lot of shit that he didn't necessarily need to take. But he was so devoted to Marvin that he took the verbal abuse with patience and good humor. Marvin would get in a mood and take it out on Elgie, just because that was the person who was closest to him. Here's a guy who's fighting all these battles by himself, and you need an outlet for those frustrations. Elgie seemed to understand that, because he wasn't just an employee, he was a friend. And the pressure was definitely building, oh yes."

It required marathon sessions to get the vocal job done, as engineer Smith remembers all too well: "We had been doing vocals for three or four days, at least 12 hours a day, and we were exhausted. I was cleaning up the tapes, and made a mistake and erased a couple of lines of Wholy Holy, just because I was so tired. Marvin fired me. He was as tired as I was, and under all this pressure – Berry was threatening him if the album wasn't finished, the film people were threatening to sue if he didn't show up on time, and the IRS was threatening him because that's what they do – and it got *very* emotional. It was four o'clock in the morning and he was crying and I was fired. I went home without a job. The next morning the office called and said, 'Pack your bags, Marvin wants you to go to LA with him.' That's how Marvin was."

When Smith mentioned this Los Angeles excursion, I always assumed he was talking about the April trip to Los Angeles to film the movie during which additional recording was done. But in subsequent conversations he indicated that this was an earlier trip, a three-day quickie undertaken prior to the mixing stage. He would have been fired on the final day of recording, March 30, and rehired for the LA trip on 31 march. Though the company logs have no record of it, it is entirely possible that they did a couple of sessions at the Sound Factory in Los Angeles before the album was mixed by Smith and Gaye back in Detroit on April 5.

With the film production looming, Marvin's presence may have been required for a day of wardrobe fitting or test shooting. With April 2 being his 32nd birthday, he may have wanted to spend it with his wife Anna, then on the Coast (and assuming that Marvin's creative high had also prompted an upswing in their roller-coaster relationship). There was the repair work to be done on

Wholy Holy, which inveterate tinkerer Marvin probably extended to other tracks as well. As Marvin was known to pay for last-minute sessions himself, such recording would not have shown up in the company logbooks.

At the Sound Factory they found a strange instrument, described by Steve Smith as "like an organ with all these unique voicings" and since identified as a Mellotron, which was added to the tag of Mercy Mercy Me. Final engineer Lawrence Miles remembers neither Steve Smith nor the Mellotron overdub, lending further credence to Smith's account. Because there is no paper trail, however, we have not included these sessions in our timeline at the back of this book.

The album, in typical Prince Of Motown fashion, was finished by the skin of his teeth. The late Thomas "Beans" Bowles liked to tell the story of getting a late-night call from the singer. His album was done, Marvin said, but there was one small part he was dissatisfied with, and needed Bowles to tweak it. The saxophonist grabbed his flute as requested, and shot over to Studio B. The place was deserted except for the singer and his engineer. Bowles blew some flute throughout the seven minutes of Right On and was out of there in under an hour.

The credited flautist disputes this story. Dayna Hartwick had been doing sessions for Motown since being recruited out of an amateur park band when she was only 13. Her first session was for Reach Out I'll Be There, and her first memory of Motown is being carried into the Snakepit by James Jamerson and Joe Messina, owing to the cast on her broken leg. She was still a teenager at the time of the *What's Going On* sessions, which she remembers with crystal clarity because Marvin Gaye asked her to do something she'd never done before.

"I had already done an overdub session for them in the afternoon to add some specific parts," she says. "Then Marvin asked me to come back later that night to do another overdub, and told me to be ready to solo. When I heard it was this jazz thing, I got *very* nervous because I'd never played that music before. I hesitated to do it because the thought made me uncomfortable. At least it was later at night, when there wasn't a room full of people. I went ahead and did it, but I could never bring myself to listen to it. Some years later a friend asked me about it, and I had to admit that I'd never heard it. I asked her how terrible it was, and she said 'not at all, it's pretty darn good actually.' That's when I finally listened, and I can tell you it's definitely me. I'm sure none of the jazz masters lost any sleep over my playing, but I think I responded pretty well to the track. I started out classically, but I was so young when I played with those great musicians that I think they had taught me to be adaptable without me being aware of it."

The album was mixed on April 5 by Steve Smith with an abundance of input from the writer/producer/ artist sitting in the chair next to him, and delivered just under the wire. Marvin headed back to Los Angeles to honor the thespian obligation from which he'd tried unsuccessfully to extricate himself, secure in the knowledge that the gift he had been given was ready to be given to the world.

8 Into The Light

*I like to take my time. I'm a perfectionist. The
people at the record company would like an album
every six months. I can never understand why
there's so much of a rush to get albums out. Do they
think I'm going to die? I figure I've got 40 years to
go. That's a lot of time to make a few more records
for them.*

Marvin Gaye

THE FINAL MIX HAD BEEN TURNED IN AND
assigned a master number, a huge relief to the people at
the company who'd been screaming for product, product,
product. But at some point in his month-plus California
stay – the exact when and why of it will probably never be

known – Marvin changed his mind. He decided his album wasn't finished after all.

The tapes were flown to Los Angeles, much to the company's distress as it had already begun printing album jackets. Before he could address their concerns, he had to first get through his second acting assignment, in the celluloid atrocity Chrome & Hot Leather. (Though Marvin had no difficulty trumpeting his imagined ability to master any discipline, athletic or aesthetic, you never heard him brag about his acting. There were two very good reasons for this; neither, thankfully, is available on home video.) Then he was free to work for another day on his lead and background vocals, adding extra texture to the blend of voices on Mercy Mercy Me, Right On, Wholy Holy and Inner City Blues. There was an additional Saturday afternoon session where trumpeter Chuck Findley and tenor sax player Bill Green were invited to improvise their way through these selections, though whether their contributions show up in the finished album is unclear.

In Motown engineering lore, a story has been passed down about the final mix of *What's Going On*. To hear the engineers tell it, Lawrence Miles became so enamored of this music that he had an epiphany about how it should sound. He felt, in that strange sonic way that engineers experience things, that he heard exactly what this music was trying to communicate, maybe more clearly than even its composer did. So one Sunday morning he snuck into the studio and locked the door behind him, keeping Marvin and everyone else out so he could follow his vision without interference. Larry's vision, they say, is the album we've been listening to for 30 years, the final flash of divine inspiration in a project peppered with little miracles.

Alas, the story turns out to be untrue. "Oh man, I wish I could tell you it was something magical like that," says Larry Miles when we finally connect with him on a cellphone heading north on the San Diego Freeway. "But there was no way to lock the world out with Marvin around. Not on this album. It was too important to him." Miles's description of the mixing process is almost identical to Steve Smith's account of the Detroit mix: the engineer would be left to put together a basic structure by himself; then he'd be joined by Marvin and the two of them would tear it down to the foundation and rebuild.

"He listened to what I'd done," Miles explains, "and said 'I like it, but it's too big,' and we began establishing what he was looking for. He wanted a certain subtlety; he didn't want it to jump out and beat you up. As he explained it, it was to be an intimate listening experience. We were mixing it for people sitting in their living rooms listening to the album straight through. He wanted to tell the story through texture applied creatively. He used the voices to color the tracks, either as texture or to emphasise some aspect of the storyline. He had so many ideas that in a couple of places we even added vocals on top of the final 2-track mix."

Though this is not quite the God-smacked mixdown of legend, we can certainly add Larry Miles to the long list of heroic improbables associated with this album. He'd gotten his engineering education in the military, working with radar and missile guidance systems. His subsequent electronics work in the private sector had been for defense contractors until he saw a newspaper ad for an opening in Motown's engineering department. He had no experience in audio engineering or music, but Mike McLean hired him anyway, on the condition that he read the Audio Encyclopedia front to back. Under the tutelage of Cal Harris, he rose from reference disc cutter to session engineer. He left Motown in '69 for Los Angeles, where he had been doing sound for network newscasts. Motown rehired him for its coastal staff not long before Marvin came out to fulfill his film obligation.

The engineer's lack of musical grounding may have worked to the advantage of *What's Going On*. The recently-unearthed Detroit mix by Steve Smith and Marvin is excellent, though a slightly rougher, more straightforward sound in which each instrument is conventionally defined. "His direction to me was to mix it as rhythmically as possible," recalls Smith. "He wanted the voices and the percussion to be emphasised, and to keep the rhythm going through it like the heartbeat of a late-night party. That was the mood he was looking to capture with me."

By comparison, the Los Angeles mix of May 6 is radical. One can point to a few specific divergences – the vocals are more layered (Smith's mix, available in the deluxe 30th anniversary double-disc edition of *What's Going On*, plays up the duet approach throughout), the party chatter is cut way back and repositioned, and while Van De Pitte's strings are emphasised, the brass is mixed into the undertow – but the real difference is more difficult to pin down. Having had time away from the rush to complete it, Marvin came back to the album with fresh ears and was unafraid to mess with it. The mission this time was not to make a record, it was to create a sonic environment and then extend it. *What's Going On* still floats in its own atmosphere, bringing intimacy to the universal, thanks in no small part to radar engineer Larry Miles.

Releasing the record, version one: "I remember that when the album was finished, Harry [Balk] ordered an initial pressing of one million albums. Harry says it wasn't that many, 300,00 or something. Whatever the number was, it was unheard-of at Motown. The sales department and the bean counters went crazy. They went over Harry's head and called Berry Gordy in LA saying, 'This guy is out of his mind, he's gonna break they company and somebody's gotta put a stop to this, buh buh buh.' So Berry called Harry, who told him, 'Look, I'll tell you what: I'll put my job on the line for this record.' He believed in the record; nowadays it's all demographics and lawyers." – Ralph Terrana, assistant to Harry Balk.

Releasing the record, version two: "Ralph's a good man, but he's got it slightly wrong. It wasn't pressings, it was album covers. I'd had that history with the single, and I'd heard other bits and pieces that I'd loved, so I took an interest and went down to Sales. I asked how many slicks [the printed cover artwork that was, in those long-ago days, pasted on to the cardboard sleeve]. When they told me 65,000 I said they were nuts, that they better order 300,000 or 400,000 to start. They said *I* was nuts, that Marvin had never sold more than 50,000 albums, even on the big ones. I told them this was going to be the biggest thing Motown had ever had, and they laughed at me. They didn't do it, and the goddamn thing was back-ordered for I don't know how long." – Harry Balk, head of the Creative Department.

Releasing the record, version three: "Harry's a wonderful guy, but he's got it all wrong. I can't imagine that we would have ordered less than 250,000 copies up-front on that album on that artist. And as far as being back-ordered . . . well, there was never a Motown record that we were back-ordered on, unless it was in the very earliest days. Not on my watch." – Barney Ales, Vice-President of Sales.

The album completed its long journey from the mind of Marvin Gaye to the record shops of America on May 21, 1971. The first time you picked up *What's Going On* you knew you were holding a very different kind of Motown album. For starters, the cover was gorgeous. To say that Motown's artwork was generally mediocre is being charitable; most of their packages looked like they'd been designed with one eye on the cutout bin. If early Motown albums were generally a hit or two and a hastily assembled gaggle of filler tracks, most got the covers they deserved.

"There was very little thought put into the

company's artwork, and it showed," contends Curtis McNair, who joined the company as Art Director in 1968. "I tried hard to up the quality of what we were putting out but it was difficult. Other labels of Motown's stature had entire art departments, but I was pretty much a one-man operation. When I got there, I could not believe how terrible so many of the covers looked, and these were some of the best records ever made. The artwork seldom did justice to the music, and that bothered me. It also bothered me that for the first year or so they wouldn't give me any credit on the albums, like they didn't want anybody to know who I was."

What's Going On deserved better, and got it. The cover shot is a simple close-up of a bearded Marvin, his black leather trenchcoat pulled up to protect him from the cold March sleet – rapidly turning to snow – that has begun to bead on his face and hair. His eyes are upturned, as if he were gazing at something out there far beyond the record racks. On the other side (also in color, unusual for a Motown rear cover) the camera has pulled back to reveal that Marvin is standing by a playground swingset, a bunch of toys piled up against the wall in back of him. It is a picture that obviously speaks to the song Save The Children, but it says much more. Marvin had vowed that he'd never again wear a suit and tie and play the plastic

Motown sharpie. But here he is in a black suit, his eyes downturned and his brow furrowed, almost as if he were attending a funeral. Which, in a way, he was. The setting suggests that he's presiding over the death of innocence, the unquestioning innocence that had created the Sound Of Young America, a phrase conspicuous in its absence from this package. It's time for Motown to put away childish things, the picture says, and take a long hard look at the world beyond the company's safe little playground.

Photographer Jim Hendin preferred to shoot in the controlled environment of his studio, but made an exception for his first session with Marvin Gaye. "He was on a strict timetable," Hendin says. "He seemed to be under a lot of pressure to get this album done. He held on to it until the very last minute, so nobody was quite sure what it was about. It was just this mysterious thing he was working on. It took some coaxing to get him to even do a photo shoot; with the album not done it was the last thing he wanted to think about. But when I got to the house, he couldn't have been more co-operative. The session took place over a couple of days. We shot inside the house with Marvin at his piano. Then I shot him outside playing basketball with his buddies, and jogging around the neighborhood. He even stopped and helped a neighbor load a moving van. We took some at a local barbershop too. The cover shots were the last ones taken. Marvin went out into his backyard, and as I clicked away it began to snow. That drizzle added everything to the shots. Luck, or something stronger, was with us that day."

Curtis McNair: "That cover almost didn't make it. I looked over the slides that came back from Jim Hendin's photo session, and selected the one that I thought would make the best cover. But my supervisor Tom Schlesinger didn't like it. Hendin had gone for a somewhat low-angle shot, and he thought it showed too much of Marvin's nostrils or something ridiculous like that. What I saw in the picture was concern, an expression on his face that tied into the questions he'd asked on the What's Going On single. Schlesinger had his own pick, and we had quite a 'debate' on the subject. But I knew that Marvin was upstairs in one of the mixing rooms, so I suggested that we go up and let the man himself make the call. We did, and Marvin backed my choice. 'This is definitely the cover right here,' he said. It took him all of five seconds to make up his mind."

Everything about the package echoed the mature intent of the music. It was a gatefold cover that opened up like a book, unheard of for a single Motown album. If you were to take The Beatles' *Sgt Pepper* cover, open its gatefold and lie it flat front cover up, it matches the inner sleeve of

Marvin's gatefold exactly: lyrics and credits on the left side, and a collage of figures on the other. Jim Hendin remembers the collage – a collection of Gaye/Gordy family photos with special emphasis on the children – as the last element, and being called upon to put it together literally overnight. Nobody remembers how it was that the company agreed to the unprecedented gatefold and the printing of the lyrics. Perhaps it had been part of Marvin's mysterious bargain with Berry Gordy back in February.

"The album was due and we didn't have the song lyrics yet," says Georgia Ward, who at that time worked in the A&R department. "Marvin was in LA doing a movie, and I was instructed to call him out there to let him know how desperately we needed them. He said he didn't have them written out, but that he could sing them if I'd take them down. I went to my boss and told her that he wanted to sing them over the telephone. She just said, 'Whatever it takes.' So I got on the phone while he sang every single song on that album. He'd sing the words, then go back and recite them to make sure I got it right. I took down everything, some in shorthand but most in long-hand, to the last 'doo doo doo.' I was on the phone for hours! I had writer's cramp and my ears were hurting but we got it done. I guess I got a Marvin Gaye concert that nobody else has gotten. I only wish that I could have sat back and enjoyed it."

(The printing of the lyrics may have been a Motown breakthrough, but it was largely symbolic, a physical means of announcing that this was music with something to say. "I respect poetry," Marvin said some years later, "and I try to write subtly, but lyrics really aren't poems. Printing them like poems can make them seem silly." If only he'd possessed such wisdom in 1971. There is much good writing and rhythmic phrasemaking in these nine songs, but the words are a dead language until Marvin's voice brings them to life. Their meaning is as much in the way the words are sung, and the way that singing is fitted into the track, as it is in the letters they employ. And it was probably not a good idea to've transcribed every last vocal vamp. Typical is Save The Children. Here is the most powerful and passionate vocal statement on the entire album, yet the last two lines of the printed lyric read, 'Oh, la, la, la, la, la, la, la / Oh, dig it everybody.")

The cover bore the notation "Orchestra Conducted and Arranged by David Van De Pitte," as if he were Nelson Riddle to Marvin's Frank Sinatra, which was not terribly far off the mark. Motown arrangers generally received no credit whatsoever, let alone front cover billing.

Motown's wall of secrecy surrounding its prized creative staffs was first breached in July 1969 and, strange as it may seem, it took an album from arch-rival Stax Records to do it. It involved the most invisible members of the Motown process, the recording engineers. One-time Motown session guitarist, producer and co-owner of Revilot Records (which had scored hits with the Parliaments and Darrell Banks) Don Davis had migrated to the Memphis soul label, but he kept his Detroit connections intact. Isaac Hayes brought the rhythm tracks for his *Hot Buttered Soul* album up to the Motor City, where strings and backing vocals were added at United Sound with engineer Ed Wolfrum, and then mixed by Russ Terrana at his brother Ralph's studio Terra Shirma. Both engineers were credited, something Motown had never seen fit to do.

Ed Wolfrum: "We all knew that little credit was going to shake things up. The reverberations from Memphis were definitely going to be felt in Detroit. At long last some recognition was involved. A good engineer should be transparent in the process – if he's doing his job you won't be aware of him at all – but that doesn't mean he should go uncredited." Excellent point. And one that Motown can't have missed, as *Hot Buttered Soul* outsold any album in their catalog. The record actually broke out of Detroit, where shops couldn't keep it in stock. Motown didn't acknowledge the breach of security until nine months later, when Norman Whitfield was permitted to credit Russ Terrana on the Temptations album *Psychedelic Shack*.

Odd, *What's Going On* did not list the engineers, an oversight Elgie Stover attributes to Marvin calling in the credits off the top of his head from an airport payphone just before boarding a flight for Los Angeles. (This has been rectified in the two-disc deluxe edition of the album released in 2001.) In every other respect, the package blew the lid off the entire system. The arranger was trumpeted on the front cover. Finally, for the first time ever on a Motown record, the contributing musicians were identified and credited, from the Funk Brothers through the Detroit Symphony string players. (Valerie Simpson released a solo album the same month which also listed musicians, but as the company preferred to see her as a writer/producer with Nick Ashford rather than a recording artist, her record sank without a trace. Simpson was finding out what it was like to be assigned a box by Motown.) Drummer Benny Benjamin, who was as responsible for the Motown sound as anyone except maybe James Jamerson, was already in his grave, but the

Funk Brothers had begun their long, slow slog toward recognition. They were Berry Gordy's secret weapons no more.

It was obvious to everyone who worked with him that Marvin's ambitions – in the musical arena, on the football field, in the bedroom – turned on delusions of grandeur. Yet even those who were not in his corner had to admit that with this album he actually lived up to his grandest delusions.

What's Going On is a triumph of sequencing. The spliced-together six-song suite on side one of the vinyl – What's Going On, What's Happening Brother, Flyin' High (In The Friendly Sky), Save The Children, God Is Love and Mercy Mercy Me (The Ecology) – flows like a dream, its twists and turns cushioned by the simultaneously lush and rhythmically enhanced surround sound. Easily and endlessly listenable, it imprints its messages, problem and solution alike, a bit more each time it is played.

Side two flows, but its three songs are also individual pieces with their own inter-relationships. It begins with the jazzy, deceptively amiable party groove of Right On and ends on the more ominous groove of Inner City Blues. Between them you have the statement of spiritual unity Wholy Holy, around which the other two songs wrap like yin and yang. Those "drowning in the sea of happiness" at the top of the side, and those drowning in despair at the other end in Inner City Blues are both positioned to receive the grace that radiates from Wholy Holy. In the midst of the Right On get-together "for those of us who simply like to socialise" comes a slower, more reflective interlude that anticipates Wholy Holy. When the drums and flute re-enter to shake us out of this reverie, we understand what the song has been about from note one: jammin' in the name of the Lord.

The brief reprise of What's Going On at the end of Inner City Blues points back to the beginning of the record, but anyone who grew up with vinyl albums and record players with repeat arms knows how easy it was to get lost in the cycles of each side. When I bought my first copy of the album it took me a good while to even get to side two. With the advent of the compact disc we can experience the entire piece with only the briefest intermission, and hear how the flute in the intro of Right On rises out of the ashes of the Mercy Mercy Me fade.

As personal meditation, *What's Going On* is as deep as Van Morrison's *Astral Weeks*. "In one way or another everything he wrote was about himself," observes Joe Schaffner. "Even What's Going On, which asks a lot of universal questions, relates to his family situation. Your mother is worried about her son being in Vietnam, because people's kids from the neighborhood are already dying over there. She can't talk to the one who's away, so she calls the only other son she has. I know their conversations went deep; because he was taking on his mother's worry on top of his own fear for Frankie's safety and outrage at the war itself. His songs were about how things emotionally affected him, and he wanted to let others who might feel the same know they weren't alone. That's how a personal feeling becomes universal."

What's Happening Brother is not just the story of a Vietnam vet back in the world, it's also about Marvin's relationship with his returning brother, and perhaps unspoken atonement for not having answered any of Frankie's letters from the war. Flying High (In The Friendly Sky) – first called So Stupid Minded and then The Junkie – was about a heroin addict, but also expressed the singer's longing to escape, and recognised his personal capacity for self-destruction, sadly foreshadowing the slave to cocaine he'd become before the decade was out. Marvin was not yet that person, but he understood how easily he could go that way. The junkie subject of the song was an anonymous burnout, not based on any specific person of their acquaintance says co-author Elgie Stover, but Marvin clearly recognised his face.

Marvin Gaye had two fathers, and he addressed

them both. The triumph of the album, and the frustration of his life, was that he had a much better relationship with his heavenly Father than with his earthly one. God is evoked throughout; the presence of Marvin Gay Sr is always there by implication, and sometimes more directly. "Father, father, we don't need to escalate" seems to speak directly to their stormy history. (Though the line could also refer to a President of the United States who kept shipping more young men off to die in Vietnam, muddying the waters with a third father figure.) There was a barbed irony in God Is Love when he sang, "Love your mother, she bore you/Love your father, he works for you," considering that the elder Gay had never supported his family financially. The Reverend had always left it to someone else – first his wife, and now Marvin – to be the breadwinner. There's another moment in an early mix of Mercy Mercy Me where Marvin's chant of "have mercy father, please have mercy father", barely audible in the finished record, seems less a prayer than the supplication of a frightened child.

As social commentary, *What's Going On* is as powerful as *There's A Riot Going On*, the Sly And The Family Stone album that came along six months later, though expressed in a very different manner. Sly Stone's title may have been an answer to Marvin's, and it feels like the San

Franciscan had taken the desolate terrain of Inner City Blues and stretched it to an album-size canvas on which he painted his bleak masterpiece. *What's Going On* lacks the jittery militancy of Sly's album. Racism doesn't rate a single specific mention, though any African-American listener understands the racism inherent in every one of the album's social scenarios. Its concerns are spiritual, economic, ecological, and its politics are largely personal in that they're seen through the eyes of the Vietnam vet (What's Happening Brother), the junkie (Flying High) and the desperately unemployed (Inner City Blues). Its most aggressive lyric, "Make me wanna holler, throw up both my hands", comes straight from the church, not the picket line or a speech by some Black Panther firebrand.

When Gaye told David Ritz that not only could he no longer sing silly love songs, neither could he sing "instant message songs", he might've been aiming his barb at the highly calculated relevance of Norman Whitfield's productions of the time. Whitfield made brilliant records, but his primary mission was to have hits, not deliver messages. "They got Western Union for that," he's reported to have sniffed when someone mistook his trend-consciousness for social commitment. He wouldn't have attempted Edwin Starr's War until it was a reasonably sure bet that popular sentiment would power such a statement to the top of the charts. "I don't like to speculate," Whitfield told Nelson George. "My thing was to revolutionise the sound . . . but without speculating." He wanted the sound of revolution without the messy, unpredictable reality of revolution itself. Whitfield's Psychedelic Shack was to true psychedelia what, say, the Supremes' The Happening was to the Exploding Plastic Inevitable. It was a longhair wig, and not always a terribly convincing one.

With the exception of Starr's thunderous War and the Temptations' bracing Cloud Nine, none of the producer's "relevant" records could hold a candle to the real Norman Whitfield/Barrett Strong benchmarks of the post-Grapevine period: Just My Imagination and Papa Was A Rolling Stone for the Tempts, and Smiling Faces for the Undisputed Truth. These are the hits that most significantly expanded the vocabulary of record production and establish Whitfield's indisputable genius. When he followed War with the utterly inferior knockoff Stop The War Now, however, this particular game was up.

Still, Norman Whitfield's ascendance meant a sea change in what people had come to take for granted as the Motown Sound. Within months of Sly Stone's rock and soul breakthrough with Dance To The Music (can't forget the Chambers Brothers' Time Has Come Today either), Whitfield had retooled the Temptations for counterculture hipness with Cloud Nine. He was aided in this by a supplemental Funk Brother with a wah wah pedal, and guitarists Dennis Coffey and Melvin "Wah-Wah Watson" Ragin. It was not the same old song, and it was not quite the same old sound.

But if Motown wished to have its soul genuinely psychedelicised, it needed look no further than its own back yard and the wild-eyed figure of George Clinton. His group the Parliaments had enjoyed a national hit with I Wanna Testify in 1967, and *really* enjoyed meeting some Harvard kids with Timothy Leary connections when their subsequent tour took them to Boston. When they brought their suddenly-expanded funk consciousness back to Detroit, the Parliaments – there was no Funkadelic yet, but crazy wheels were definitely turning – found a willing audience among the city's hippies, sharing stages (as well as various herbal and/or chemical sacraments) with rock groups like Iggy Pop's notorious Stooges, the rabble-rousing MC5, and Ted Nugent's Amboy Dukes. The black music establishment thought Clinton had lost his mind, to which he'd have happily agreed. George had briefly been a Jobete songwriter when the Parliaments were still living in New Jersey, but the marriage never stood a chance – it was lava lamp oil and water.

George Clinton: "When it came to the radio, they could tell us our new thing was too white for black people. Then the others would say it was too black for white people. Truth is, it was too *freaky* for all of 'em. But in [black] clubs we didn't have that problem because we played such funky music, and we did such crazy things on stage that we were a novelty. We were like Halloween; it was a holiday every time we played. To them we were clowning, like a psychedelic Coasters or something. I remember Berry Gordy's wife and sisters coming into the Twenty Grand club wearing their minks. I would walk across their table buck nekkid, pour wine on my head and let it drip all the way down to my dick. Motown had gotten so slick and sophisticated – everything led to the Copacabana, the elephant graveyard. But as individuals the Motown people needed it and enjoyed it. They were ready to break out of that mold and cut loose.

"We used to laugh at Norman Whitfield. He'd come into the Twenty Grand, set up his recorder on a table right in front of us and tape the show. It's well known. He'll tell you, Stevie Wonder, everybody from Motown will tell you. Melvin Franklin [of the Temptations] would call us two days later and say [deep bass voice] 'Hey George, you know that riff y'all play, *da da dadumda*? Norman just cut it.' But that's not really stealing as far as I'm concerned. Those vibrations were out there in the air to be shared; that was the whole point. We were just trying to spread it around. What bothers me about records like Cloud Nine and Psychedelic Shack was that he made them without any commitment to, or awareness of, what the kids were trying to say with that music. It's like doing magic with your left hand; it backfires on you for real. Norman would wear all of us out for doing drugs, but he had the biggest habit in the world: gambling. And now he lives in Vegas! That's like moving into the dope man's house. I tease him about that whenever I see him."

The difference between Whitfield and *What's Going On* was conscience. Norman's records were the product of cultural awareness, Marvin's new kind of soul music came from the soul itself. Marvin's question "What's going on?" was to black music what Bob Dylan's "How does it feel?" had been to rock'n'roll a half-decade earlier: a new consciousness examining itself musically. The removal of the question mark Obie Benson had originally affixed to the title may be intentional, issued as Marvin's challenge to Motown to deal with the reality it presents: this *is* what's going on.

*

Gordy had released albums of Martin Luther King speeches during the civil rights struggles of the early '60s. Langston Hughes poetry and Stokely Carmichael harangues appeared on the short-lived Black Forum label in the early '70s, but this venture proved to be more talk than action, and was certainly not intended to provoke Motown's musical artists into thinking for themselves politically. But even if Marvin's album represents the company's true social breakthrough, it serves mainly to reinforce how isolated the magical Motown kingdom had been from the real world.

Socio-political content had been a force in mainstream pop long before the dawn of the rock era, two touchstones being Billie Holiday's Strange Fruit in 1939 and the Weavers' bringing of Woody Guthrie to the hit parade with So Long (It's Been Good To Know Ya) in 1951. Motown's entry with the Valadiers' Greetings (This Is Uncle Sam) looks promising on paper, but this 1961 conscription lament by the label's first white group was played for teen angst and Coasters-style humor, even when covered by the Monitors five years later as the war in Vietnam raged. Stevie Wonder's 1966 cover of Blowin' In The Wind had been considered daring within Motown, and while it did take Dylan to the top of the soul charts, its singalong syncopation also robbed the song of its mysterious edge. (Though, to be fair to Little Steveland, folkie overexposure had already ruined the song, turning it into a misinterpreted feelgood lullaby.)

Marvin was not exactly up-to-the-moment himself. The long hair he sings about in the title song had largely ceased to be an issue, and the street phrases he turned into song titles Right On and What's Happening Brother were already borderline clichés. Motown didn't get around to releasing its first true '60s-style album until 1971, but it may be precisely because of the company's reality lag that songs like Flying High, Mercy Mercy Me and especially Inner City Blues offered a hard look at what was waiting on the other side of those shimmering '60s daydreams. *What's Going On* wasn't really topical – about its time – at all. It was about the future:

> *Crime is increasing*
> *Trigger happy policing*
> *Panic is spreading*
> *God knows where we're heading*
> *Make me wanna holler, the way they do my life . . .*

The greatness of *What's Going On* is not simply that it paints pictures of socio-economic desperation contemporary eyes still recognise, but that it offers something beyond platitude to hang on to. Its faith in the life of the spirit, which animates the music even when the lyric is articulating the problem, makes the album something more than the "black *Sgt Pepper*" it is often described as. In its musical maturity and stylistic cohesion it can be better compared to the Beach Boys' *Pet Sounds*, and the delight of the LA session musicians called the Wrecking Crew in Brian Wilson's music mirrors the response of the Funk Brothers to Marvin's. And it goes *Pet Sounds* one better by also fulfilling the aim of Wilson's abandoned would-be masterwork *Smile*: it is a pop symphony to God. Journey To The Sky was one of the first songs Marvin learned and performed as a child. It was his mother's favorite, and Marvin's visionary album can be seen as his own version of that old gospel plough.

As spiritual expression *What's Going On* is closest of all to John Coltrane's *A Love Supreme*, the 1964 jazz album in which the Master's hand moves through the saxophonist's quartet to offer nourishment to all who will open themselves to it. Marvin's masterwork demands a similar openness, though his is emotional more than musical, and offers the same food for the soul. The smooth swagger of his best singing is muted; here he has the humility of a messenger. "To be truly righteous," he explained to biographer David Ritz, "you offer love with a pure heart, without regard for what you'll get in return. I had myself in that frame of mind. People were confused and needed reassurance. God was offering that reassurance through his music. I was privileged to be the instrument."

Unlike *Astral Weeks* and *A Love Supreme*, where abstraction was the key to their ability to evoke, Marvin was plain-speaking to the point of bluntness. Though not militant, his album is unmistakably a call to action, or perhaps a call to awareness. Yet he cedes no ground to either of those recordings in terms of mystery or mysticism, because what he offered was the forthrightness, and transcendence, of gospel music. There has never been a Marvin Gaye album with less sex than *What's Going On*, but few records by anybody have contained more love.

"I've always looked at this record as the true successor to A Change Is Gonna Come," remarks critic Dave Marsh, an observation that is on the money in many ways. Sam Cooke sang, "It's been too hard living but I'm afraid to die/Because I don't know what's up there beyond the sky," and Marvin sensed a similar fatigue and uncertainty in the human community surrounding him. But he, like Cooke, knew exactly what lay beyond the cloud cover, and for this shining moment saw clearly the strength it could provide in the continuing struggle to survive in a world to which that change has not yet come.

Sam Cooke was a singer Marvin had always admired – as a vocal stylist, as a man of style, and most especially as someone who'd left church music for success in the pop mainstream but had found in A Change Is Gonna Come a meaningful way to bridge the gap and reconnect with the spirit. (In a spooky coincidence, Marvin had assumed some of the live dates left open when Cooke was fatally shot on December 11, 1964, and was then briefly discussed as a possible candidate to portray the late singer in a big-screen biopic that remains unmade.) With *What's Going On* Gaye achieves the combination of moral conviction and vocal ease that drives Cooke's eternal classic. Like Sam's song, Marvin's album suite offers solace, and resolve, on whatever level one approaches it – social, political, spiritual or musical. Had Cooke lived long enough to hear it, he would surely have praised the Lord for the way Marvin made gospel forms and sentiments secular without sacrificing one iota of righteousness. Here is Dr King's "weapon of love" wielded through music.

Ed Wolfrum: "I think God gave him this project to do. There was a deep spiritual side to Marvin that he didn't always choose to bring forth. I think he'd finally owned up to that. He *had* to tell this story. Everybody who worked with him on this project will tell you that he was a driven man. There was something that needed to be said, and only he could say it in quite this way. What was inspiring him can be put down to a number of factors, but my belief is that God had given him a job to do, and he knew it."

On one level, *What's Going On* is about the loss of innocence – in the culture, on the streets and in the music of Motown. But, even in the full face of that loss, innocence is replaced by something just as pure: faith, an all-encompassing faith that transcends innocence *and* experience. He knew that no matter how dark a picture he painted with Inner City Blues – and it is truly the Great Society's boulevard of broken dreams, with all the street-lights shot out – there was a light that could reach into its darkest corners.

Yet for an album that mentions Jesus as much as any contemporary Christian rock group, it is not directed at Jesus freaks or even Christians, Pentecostal or otherwise. Marvin is speaking through his own Bible-based experience, but his intent was to speak to the faith of all people regardless of religious affiliation. In telling these stories he hoped to awaken the spiritual voice in those who'd lost touch with theirs or perhaps had never connected with it in the first place. His grasp of root morality transcends any particular doctrine; one doesn't even need to believe in God to receive these life lessons. When, in the middle of an album that showcases the smoothest singing of his career to that point, he suddenly lets loose and shouts "Save the babies! Save the babies!" he touches something at the core of all life.

Most tellingly, *What's Going On* was a better sermon than any his father had ever preached.

"Enraptured by God" is the way Marvin Pentz Gay Sr described his youthful connection with religion. It also describes his son's experience with this album. It was not about resolving his tangled contradictions, but about setting them aside long enough to let something else come through. He took on the problems of the world as a respite from his own. His inner turmoil would dog him all his days, from which this period would prove to be no more than a temporary reprieve. Marvin Gaye was a holy artist, but he was also a deeply flawed human being. This in no way diminishes the enduring musical and spiritual power of *What's Going On*.

In one of those rare instances where a unique vision intersects with a willing public, the album was a resounding success in the marketplace. Marvin's sermon stayed on the charts for a year, peaking at Number 1 R&B

and Number 6 pop. (This caught Motown by surprise, but the album would then do something that totally confounded the singles-oriented company: It kept selling, and continues to sell a few more copies every day, to a combination of people purchasing their umpteenth copy and those who've just discovered it.)

The music press was surprised and delighted. "There are very few performers who could carry a project like this off. I've always admired Marvin Gaye, but I didn't expect that he would be one of them," admitted Vince Aletti in his Rolling Stone review. "Guess I seriously underestimated him. It won't happen again." The only conspicuously dissenting voice belonged to Robert Christgau, who graded the album no better than a B in his Village Voice record roundup. "Like any Berry Gordy quickie," he wrote, "it's baited skimpily," and labeled Van De Pitte's strings "the lowest kind of movie-background dreck". He was wrong on both counts, and his upping of the rating to a B+ in the book of his collected reviews still falls a full grade short.

For an album that the company brass had found so wildly unconventional and weird, *What's Going On* spawned three hit singles, as Mercy Mercy Me and an edited Inner City Blues followed the title track into the rarefied air at the top of the charts.

The second and third singles were as astonishing over Top 40 airwaves as What's Going On had been. Mercy Mercy Me (The Ecology) tells a story that requires no metaphor; corruption of the earth *is* the moral corruption of man. "How much more abuse from man can she stand?" is a question that, frighteningly, scientists are now beginning to answer. It was about the only irresistibly swingin' hit single I can remember from 1971 whose subject matter included nuclear holocaust, oil spills, acid rain, and fish poisonously full of mercury. Compared to apocalyptic hit parade hokum like Eve Of Destruction and In The Year 2525, Marvin's gentle, melodic chiding seems divinely restrained, a message you ask to have whispered into your ear again and again.

(This is an appropriate place to make a correction. The story has long been told that when encountering the word "ecology" in this song title, Berry Gordy had to have its meaning explained to him. Further research reveals that Gordy entered into a brief co-venture with Sammy Davis Jr called Ecology Records in 1970, so the term had at last floated across his desk.)

The brooding Inner City Blues was an even more unlikely 45, but for two factors. The rhythmic pull of the track is undeniably dark, but the way Bob Babbitt's bass plays against the percussion is hypnotic. It makes it impossible to turn away from the harsh realities Marvin lays out, which are themselves made engaging by the album's best lyric writing. "Money, we make it/'Fore we see it, you take it" and "Natural fact is/I can't pay my taxes" are not simply clever word constructions, they are so attuned to the nuances of Marvin's singing voice that it sounds as if they were composed aurally rather than worked out on paper.

What's Going On even got play on many hip FM rock radio stations, entirely new territory for Motown.

WABX-FM, home of the Air Aces, was Detroit's original underground station. "We played everything in God's creation *except* Motown," the late broadcaster Dave Dixon once told me. "It was as a reaction to how relentlessly their stuff was played everywhere else. You could spin the dial at any given time and find several stations playing Motown music." This was especially true in Detroit, but expressed the general feeling of the national FM rock community. It was one more barrier broken by *What's Going On*.

"This was one of those records that wasn't going to be denied," says Dan Carlisle, the ABX Air Ace who first played it late one evening early in June 1971. "I knew once my listeners heard it everything would be OK, but I had to set it up properly. I told them that I was about to play a major artist who's going his own way, and that this album was going to revolutionise black music like The Beatles had done for rock with *Sgt Pepper*. Then we played the album straight through, with only a break to change sides, and I didn't receive a single negative call. People loved it. It was unique new music, and that's exactly what we were supposed to be exposing our listeners to. I know other FM stations played it but it was especially important to us, because it was our Detroit roots taken to a completely different place. When we found out that it was an act of rebellion against the Motown machine, that appealed to us too."

The three singles continue to be perennials on American radio, though in a time of rigid formating and market fragmentation there are too few stations with the freedom to play the entire album. One illustrious radio broadcaster who has insisted on this freedom is the delightfully unpredictable, thought-provoking maverick who calls himself The Electrifying Mojo. Complete airings of *What's Going On* have been a staple of his programs for the past three decades, which begins to explain why, despite consistently high ratings and audience feedback, he has done his delightfully unpredictable thing for too many radio stations to list.

"I've probably played the album in its entirety as often as most people have played the single," Mojo attests when we track him down to a location he prefers to keep private. "People always call, many of them in tears at experiencing the beauty and truth for the first time. The music connects with your soul. The most amazing reactions come from children and young people, who find it daring and breathtaking and bold, and wonder why they haven't heard the whole piece before. What a ringing statement this album made, and makes. People are mesmerised – young and old, black and white, rich and poor. There were almost no demographic barriers that it couldn't overcome.

"I think Marvin Gaye was probably *born* to make *What's Going On*; that was his mission here. I always say that for Marvin this album was like getting a high-five from God. He was given this assignment from above, and in his dedication to the task he exceeded it. And when God looked back and saw how Marvin went beyond what He had asked him to do, he said 'Gimme five.' It's an album that's forever new, a continuing message to the human family."

As Marvin told the Washington Post the following year when the city hosted a "Marvin Gaye Day" for its native son and he performed the complete *What's Going*

On album live for the one and only time: "A lot of people have talked about the album in terms of it being a black record. Now, obviously, as a black man, there are things about my ethnicity that are going to come through my music. In fact, I'm bothered by the dilution that's occurring in black music today. It's getting watered down into a homogenised kind of American music and we're losing touch with the styles of people, like Muddy Waters and Jimmy Reed, who really started rhythm and blues. But I conscientiously avoided using the word 'black' on the entire record. I didn't want the album to appear to be addressed only to blacks. I was writing and singing about all people and that's the audience I was reaching for."

Here was a music that would have made Walt Whitman's heart sing with joy had he heard its open embrace, its desire to include everything, bad as well as good, about the American experience as Marvin Gaye perceived it. "I wanted to come up with something that could be translated into any language and still retain its meaning," he said, but the uniqueness of what was created 30 years ago has never required any translation at all.

The little boy who sang Journey To The Sky in a storefront church and had visions of moving millions with the sound of his voice had done it. The mighty machinery that powered him as a star had been bent through inspiration, cunning and will to serve this mission. Though *What's Going On* was the product of Marvin's fight against the company and even the Motown Sound itself, the album Berry Gordy didn't want may be the truest expression of the founder's desire to produce music that would appeal to everybody everywhere, his demographic dream come true.

But Mr Gordy was far too preoccupied elsewhere to ponder this or any other such ironies.

9 Here In The Going, Going, Gone

Berry thought like an oil man. Drill as many holes as you can and hope for at least one gusher. He wound up with a whole oil field.

Marvin Gaye

MOST ACCOUNTS PEG THE FIRST SERIOUS rupture of the Motown spirit to the company's late-1967 move from Hitsville to an office building at 2547 Woodward Avenue. There was no doubt that the operation had outgrown its home, even when Gordy acquired three other houses on West Grand Boulevard to accommodate the overflow. The Donovan Building was technically a bit closer to the center of town, but the ugly 10-storey concrete cube on a dead stretch of Woodward overlooking the Edsel Ford freeway was miles away from the company employees felt they'd been working for. It was officially called The Motown Center, but nothing about it felt like Motown, so many still referred to it as the Donovan Building, or just Woodward. "It was formerly a Welfare Department building and that's what we called it too," laughs Richard Morris without much mirth.

Elgie Stover: "As long as they were on West Grand Boulevard it was a family operation, and part of a real neighborhood. That all changed when they moved to the Donovan Building. There wasn't no place to play, no place to meet. It was in a part of town where not much was happening, so there was no interest for any of us to go over unless it was our job to be there. Everybody was on different floors in their own offices. It was a place for businessmen and secretaries, not artists and musicians."

The cold, drab building's sole concession to creativity were the mixing rooms on floors nine and ten that helped ease the burden on studios A and B. Activity at the Hitsville house continued, centering on the Snakepit, where most of the label's great basic tracks were still cut, and the tape library that cataloged the company's greatness. But now there was something new and strange in the air whenever Detroiters drove past 2648 West Grand Boulevard – a bittersweet whiff of nostalgia.

Even more problematic was the absence of the man at the top. For most Motowners the record company was a dream come true. So many people had migrated to Detroit seeking opportunity, and Motown seemed the fullest flowering of what that could mean. (A life on the assembly line, the only other viable avenue, was considerably less appealing in the boom years than it had been in post-depression America.) What very few of them understood was that it was only part of Berry Gordy's dream. He was driven to test himself in the arenas of film and television, ambitions he'd been proclaiming publicly as far back as 1961, a fact his detractors would conveniently forget. Seduced by the warm California lifestyle and pushed by the relentless ambition of his paramour Diana Ross, he never really moved into the refurbished "Gordy Manor" on Boston Boulevard. That was his showplace, but from 1967 his residence, for all intents and purposes, was Los Angeles.

Maxine Powell, who came to Motown in 1964 to create the only finishing school that ever existed within a record company ("Buckingham Palace and the White House, that's what I trained them for") was present when Berry told his mother he was leaving: "We were in his bedroom and I was visiting with Mrs Gordy, when he came in and said to her, 'Mother, I am planning to move to California.' Now, he loved the record business and he did great things there and helped hundreds and hundreds of people, but he wanted to move on, move up with something different. He told her he had to be closer to where these things happen. He said she was not to worry; she would always be looked after, and he would be back all the time, so it would hardly seem like he was gone at all."

Artie Fields, however, quickly felt something amiss. "Berry sent a few people he was grooming over to me," the studio owner explains. "He wanted to see if they had any promise as commercial singers. I pulled it together and sold the clients on it. But when I went back to Motown and had to go through six layers of management, we were never able to close the deal. Berry was already out of reach in California. But I believe that if he'd been there the deal would have been done in a day.

"I had a funny experience with him not long after. I wanted a certain singer for a Chevrolet commercial, and I called over to the office. They gave me the number on the Coast, so I called and left a message out there. No call-back. Meantime the situation obviously blew over. One Sunday afternoon six months later I get a call at home from Berry: 'Hi Artie, how's the family, how's the kids? What is it you need?' By then I couldn't even remember what I was trying to reach him for. We chatted for a half hour and hung up."

Those interpersonal relationships were what had given the company its character. "Everybody always dumped on Motown," the late Robert White told Dr Licks. "Nobody ever talks about how they bailed people out of jail, or how many times they'd pay off mortgages when people were about to lose their house. Those things never get mentioned." White was absolutely right, but those situations tend to arise naturally out of the closeness people develop in the early stages of an enterprise. It is equally natural that as the the enterprise grows so does the distance between those parties. In the case of Motown, however, this process was hastened by the main man's Coastal remove.

Berry Gordy had built and maintained Motown's magnificent system in part by being the only one seeing the larger picture, and by supplying the grease to keep his individual cogs meshing smoothly. But when he began spending a disproportionate amount of attention on only one part of his larger picture – the equally driven Miss Ross, who was cutting the Supremes loose and being groomed for solo superstardom and a parallel career as a movie star – is where we must mark the beginning of his record empire's decline. Without Gordy's unifying presence and personal involvement, back at home the grease began to harden into walls that would isolate the individual cogs and turn interaction into friction and faction.

Even when he was in town, Mr Gordy (as he quite rightly insisted upon being referred to, a formality that would eventually escalate to "The Chairman") was difficult to get to. Earl Van Dyke used to say that the problem at Motown wasn't Berry; who could be counted on to resolve any dispute fairly and squarely. As the company grew, the problem became the number of people you had to go through to get to him. That most of them were now Caucasian mattered less than the *kind* of white people they were.

Ivy Jo Hunter: "When you bring in business people who have no experience on the creative side, it becomes about the efficiency of buy and sell, and no more. It had nothing to with the human element. But music is *all about* the human element, so if you don't know how to deal with that, you're in the wrong business, buddy. Because everything that came through there started with those creative people; the numbers don't come in until the end. I knew these people were not gonna be able to run the company in the absence of the charisma of Berry Gordy. I'm looking at these guys, and I'm looking at their middlemen, and none of them know music. And the people who *do* know music are getting pushed further and further away from the source."

The somber mood on Woodward Avenue would occasionally be shattered by a visit from The Curse-Out Man. "I got fired and rehired by the company more times than I can remember," laughs Elgie Stover, still hyper-ebullient after all these years. "When Fuller Gordy asked Gwen why they kept me around, she say, 'He'll curse out the people we want cursed out.' I'd walk around that building drunk and curse *all of 'em* out. Ed Pollock [the head of finance] tried to hide whenever he saw me coming, because he knew I'd go in there and curse him out good. I'd be drunk and people would say, 'Why don't you get rid of that boy?' Gwen Gordy would say, 'Because he be doing what we wish *we* could do.' I was The Curse-Out Man, and I didn't give a damn." (For the record, Elgie wasn't always drunk and cursing. He was considered responsible enough to serve both of Berry Gordy's parents in a variety of capacities.)

But every space attracts the vibrations it deserves, and there were more fearful things roaming the corridors of the Donovan Building than the Curse-Out Man. Like the gentleman who called himself Abdullah, whose strange, intense association with Motown lasted but a matter of months in 1968. He was said to have walked from New York City to Detroit, carrying only a battered guitar, to bring his message of Afrocentric self-awareness and pride to Berry Gordy and the Motown family at the world-famous Hitsville. When his footsteps led him instead to the 10-storey tower on Woodward, where a few grinning white devils appeared to be calling the shots and signing the checks in Mr Gordy's absence, the practiced astrologer Abdullah should have sensed that the stars were seriously out of alignment. But, as his other message was that he had been anointed to become the greatest star in the Motown firmament, he decided to stick around.

Based on the recorded evidence, this was unlikely to come to pass. But what the former Joseph McLean of Brooklyn, New York, lacked in musical grace he made up for in self-confidence, and he actually talked himself into a songwriter's contract, and from there into the studio. "He was very arrogant and hot-headed," Hank Cosby remembers, "but also very creative. He wasn't really much of a singer, but lyrically and melodically he had something going on. He'd sit there for hours and strum his little guitar and sing you all these songs he'd written. Frank Wilson and I were both quite taken by him."

Taken *in* by him, some at the company said, and most tended to give the tall, intense young man a wide berth. He had apparently converted to Islam during a prison stretch, but appeared to be the sole proprietor of a sect that had as much to do with Abdullah as with the Prophet Elijah Muhammad, and was equal parts astrology, Koran, and his own poetic expression. He prayed four times a day, and was known to roll out his prayer rug in the middle of a session. He wouldn't allow women near drums, claiming their menstruation drained the instrument of its power.

Hank Cosby: "He was very difficult to work with in the studio. He'd obviously had some prior experience, but it was probably street-level, because he didn't know basic things like keeping tempo or changing key. You never knew when he was going to change key because he wasn't aware of the concept. It was rough trying to write charts around that, and damn near impossible to make it work with our rhythm section. There were constant disagreements because even though he didn't know much about music, he had very particular ideas about *his* music, and he'd object loudly to anything he didn't understand."

Difficult as it may have been, Cosby and Frank Wilson managed to record almost an album's worth of material by the irascible artist. The single I Comma Zimba Zio (Here I Stand The Mighty One) b/w Why Them, Why

Me was released in late October '68 on the Soul label. It is not a great record, and was certainly no chart contender, but is remarkable nonetheless. The top side was a percussive, chant-based expression of pride in his African heritage and dismay at what had been visited upon it: "I come from the land of a Zulu / I come from the land of a beautiful Zulu / I come from the land of a prostrated Zulu." The flip, despite its soft rhythm and sweet string arrangement, is equally uncompromising, asking why young black men should be shipped off to Vietnam (actually mentioned by name!) when they're already fighting a war at home. Powerful messages both, undercut only by the thin, unconvincing voice of the artist himself. Considering how much trouble Marvin Gaye would encounter when attempting to portray social realities in song two years later, it is remarkable that this record slipped by the Quality Control sentries and reached the outside world at all.

The Abdullah single came and went so quickly that co-producer Hank Cosby didn't even remember that it had been released. This could not have sat well with the man who'd proclaimed that he was destined to be Motown's greatest star and lead the company into a new age. Raynoma Gordy Singleton's book quotes him complaining that he was being followed by agents of the blue-eyed devils at the Donovan Building, and threatening to kill them.

Upset about money he felt was owed him – or perhaps, like any artist with a stiff record, it was about the lack of promotional attention his great artistry was being subjected to – Abdullah marched into Ralph Seltzer's office unannounced and launched into a verbal assault at maximum volume that was soon doubled by the devil's responses. Abdullah snapped, and flew across Seltzer's desk with the intention of inflicting severe bodily harm upon the small Jewish bureaucrat. He was pulled off before any real damage could be done, but in the scuffle his guitar case opened and out popped not his little guitar but a rather large machete. He'd bought a machete to deal with Berry Gordy's hachet man! Selzer was unmoved by the poetry of this gesture. Joseph McLean was given a hastily-drawn release, a little money, and a ticket on the next flight back to New York. That was the last Motown heard of Abdullah.

Hank Cosby: "Well, there were probably a lot of people who sympathised with him on that one. Ralph Seltzer was not very well liked, because he did all the dirty work for Mr Gordy. You have to excuse some of the things a person in that position does – they're only doing what they're told. My problem with him was that he got so he *enjoyed* his job. He liked it a little too much for my liking. There was a constant tenseness within the company that hadn't been there before."

The next conspicuous rupture in the Motown system was sugar-coated. It arrived in 1969 in the unlikely guise of five personable brothers from Gary, Indiana, an industrial city not far from Detroit. The fiction would be hatched that the Jackson 5 had been discovered by Diana Ross, but the truth was that the scouting reports had come in from other Motown artists, first Gladys Knight and then Bobby Taylor. The kid band (pint-sized tornado Michael Jackson was all of nine) was introduced to the company in a showy reception at the Gordy Manor. But for the all-important Motown job of artist development, they were quickly whisked off to California.

Deke Richards ran the creative division of the LA office at this time. He was road guitarist with writing and producing aspirations when he first met Berry Gordy. The Motown boss made an intuitive decision to give the green young white kid a shot, much as he'd taken executive chances with Barney Ales and Suzanne DePasse that paid off handsomely for the company. Richards made regular trips to Detroit to see how the company worked, most notably the weekend in 1968 when he and a creative think tank assembled by Gordy holed up in a suite at the

Ponchartrain Hotel and wrote Love Child to relaunch Diana Ross And The Supremes in the wake of Holland-Dozier-Holland's litigious departure. But that had happened in Detroit, and Richards wanted the LA office to have its own identity.

"I had just brought Freddie Perren and Fonce Mizell into the company," he says. "Our styles meshed, and I explained to them that the best way for us to make our mark within the company was to find a cold artist and have a hit with them. That attracts attention, as well as insuring that the act will be receptive and co-operative. We were working on a track we called I Want To Be Free that we intended for Gladys Knight. When I saw the Jackson 5 at the Daisy club in Beverly Hills, Berry said he hadn't heard the right song to launch them with, and suggested that our Gladys tune might be better suited to the kids.

"I suggested that Berry become actively involved, and that's how the four of us became the team we called the Corporation. I wanted Berry on board because nobody knew better what a hit was, but also as a hedge against any prejudice we might encounter from the home office. The Detroit people thought we were shit, some kind of tax write-off, so we all wanted to show them something. It's funny, but there were never any negatives from the black people at the company. Most of the resistance I felt was more from certain white people in administrative positions. They had their little territory carved out, and I guess I was perceived to be a threat."

Richards had studied the placement of instruments in the Snakepit, and noted the resonance of the wood floor Pops Gordy had installed. Back in Los Angeles, he attempted his own version of room identity at Dave Hassinger's Sound Factory, going so far as to build a wooden drum riser for extra resonance. His studio band, which he put on a retainer in the hope that they'd hold together like the Funk Brothers, consisted of guitarists David T. Walker, Don Peake and Louie Shelton, Wilton Felder on bass and Joe Sample on keyboards (both from the Jazz Crusaders), Joe Clayton on congas, Sandra Crouch on tambourine, and drummers Gene Pello and Ed Greene. It was a hot band but, where the Funk Brothers had lasted a generation, this aggregation held together for exactly two Jackson 5 singles. This was LA, where there were always other options.

When the retooled and retitled I Want You Back reached Number 1 early in 1970, setting off an unprecedented run of four consecutive number ones by this new act, it was a ringing triumph for Motown entering the new decade, but an ominous development for the folks back home. Here was an act put together with no input from Detroit's fabled Artist Development, not recorded in the legendary Snakepit, without the presence of a single Funk Brother – and not simply with Berry Gordy's approval, but with his hands-on involvement. The project, which could almost have been called "The Sound Of Younger America", was suddenly not only Motown's top attraction, it was the hottest thing in the entire record business. Whoever "they" may have been, they were right in perceiving a West Coast threat.

But, with business already booming in the Norman Whitfield era, the sunny California threat embodied by the Jackson 5 was written off by most Detroiters as an aberration, just another sign that Motown magic was boundless. Its seriousness was first noted by the engineers. "Pieces of our equipment began disappearing," Bob Ohlsson remembers. "And they'd say, 'Well, we're doing more and more recording in LA these days . . .'. Guy Costa had become Vice-President of Engineering out there, and a lot of us believe he was instrumental in engineering the move. It felt like he was out to sabotage the Detroit operation, and was already scavenging our stuff for his own use."

Uriel Jones: "We knew something was up when they started cutting in California. They would send some of these tapes back for us to overdub certain things, but then after awhile they had a whole crew out there to do it. There was still plenty of recording going on in Detroit, but we could feel it beginning to cut into our workload. They were cutting good stuff out there – can't argue with that – but it wasn't the Motown Sound. How could it be?" A memo dated April 10, 1970 and addressed to "All Motown Record Corp. employees" from Vice President and General Manager Barney Ales stated: "Rumors are flying. This letter is to let you know the facts. It is true that we are in a cost-cutting and economy program. The purpose is to increase company efficiency and stability." He goes on to say: "Another rumor is that the company is moving to California. This rumor is untrue. The Detroit offices are, and will remain, the home office of our company. Expended operations are taking place in California, which add to the overall diversification and therefore the overall stability and progress of our company, to the benefit of all of us. Motown Record Corporation *is not moving* to the West Coast."

If there was any doubt about where the company was headed, it was signed, sealed and delivered the day Mr Gordy was offered the leading role for Miss Ross in Lady Sings The Blues, the film version of the Billie Holiday story. From then on he had even less to do with the day-to-day running of Motown Records, yet he was every bit as hungry and driven as the young man who set out to conquer the world of music. Except that Berry Gordy Jr was no longer that wide-eyed, inexperienced young man.

"I saw him just be *electric* at a meeting with Paramount Pictures in Los Angeles," says Andrew Loog Oldham with awe 30 years later. "It was 14 white guys from Paramount on one side, and Berry and Suzanne DePasse on the other. They were telling him how the film business worked. He sat back and let them bury themselves, and then he told them how the film business was going to work for *him*. They came in thinking they were going to put this upstart in his place, and he took over the film. He was talking down to *them*. It was a wonderful moment. He flashed me one little look, the only time he acknowledged my presence, just to make sure I'd witnessed his performance. I was seeing Berry Gordy at his best."

Back in Detroit, *What's Going On* let the creative genie out of the Hitsville bottle, just as Marvin hoped it would. Never again would a Motown artist who truly had something to say be prevented from saying it simply because "that's not the way we do things here."

Everyone who recorded for the company from that moment forward reaped the benefit, but the artist who most immediately benefited was Stevie Wonder. No longer Little, his own bid for artistic recognition, the self-produced *Where I'm Coming From*, had been released the month before *What's Going On*. It and its successor *Music Of My Mind* have their moments, but they are only the distant thunder before the mighty lightning to come. Marvin's album, which he could easily have called *Music Of My Soul*, upped the ante. Not only did it emerge from freedom of expression, it had something profound to express. Stevie Wonder turned 21 the week before *What's Going On* hit the street, and the liberation in Marvin's music was reflected in the contractual assurance of full creative control that the adult Wonder renegotiated for himself. Stevie didn't come into full possession of his own creative voice until *Talking Book* in 1973, but Marvin's inspiration suffuses that three-album process.

Marvin Gaye had succeeded in ushering in a new era on the assembly line. *What's Going On*, the first Motown hit to list the names of the musicians who made it, was a coming-out for the Funk Brothers that had been a long time coming. What the utterly vindicated and thoroughly delighted Gaye could never have anticipated was that, as the last great album recorded in Detroit before the company left town for good, it turned out to be the musicians' swansong as well.

10 Can't Forget The Motor City?

You know I'll always take care of you.

Berry Gordy Jr

"IN 1966 I POSED A QUESTION TO THOSE brown-nosers the Funk Brothers," Jack Ashford remembers with a dismissive snort, though the percussionist is himself a key member of the Brotherhood. "It was Eddie Bongo, Earl Van Dyke, Robert White and Pistol Allen. I said, 'What would happen if Berry decided to shut this shit down tomorrow?' They looked at me like I was crazy. 'We're the hottest thing in the business, nobody's gonna mess with us,' and so forth. The reason that I asked this question was that, in my observance of Berry Gordy at a distance, how he treated people was reminiscent of the hustlers I used to see coming up in Philadelphia – sporting people, the numbers guys, the players. I don't necessarily mean this in a negative way; hustlers are the ones who make things happen. So I knew that with a guy like Berry, things were never gonna stand still. Remember, the Roman Empire fell, and that was bigger than anything. The guys laughed, but that's exactly what happened. They shut it down on 'em, saying, 'We're gonna reschedule this date next week.' Next week hasn't come yet."

It wasn't only the musicians who were caught off guard by a move that, though rumored for some time, seemed impossible to conceive of. Martha Reeves got the news when she returned from maternity leave. "I had my mandatory month's rest after the delivery," she remembers. "I called to get the next instructions for me and the group. I wanted to report for work, and was told there was nothing scheduled for me. I asked to speak to Berry Gordy, but they said he'd moved to California permanently a couple of months before my delivery. I was told, 'Girl, don't you know we've moved? As soon as this equipment cools down it'll all be shipped to Los Angeles and the company will be gone for good.' I had no idea they were moving! And of all the people – I thought I had sold enough records to have earned the respect of some notification. I helped *start* the company, and not to be even informed? Evidently Berry Gordy's people weren't taking care of the business that he assigned to them. Mr Gordy is just not that kind of person."

The company employees learned about it the same day the public did. "We'd hear little rumblings," says Georgia Ward, "but we were always told that, no, the company was not moving to LA. Don't believe the rumors. Mr Gordy just wants to maintain a home here and a home out there, nothing more. That was a great relief to us. We had such a good thing going, and so successful, that why would you uproot and move away? People could not really believe that this would happen. Then one day we were at the office with the radio on, when all of a sudden we were hearing the voice of Ewart Abner and he was making the announcement that Motown would be officially moving to Los Angeles! It wasn't a total surprise because of what we'd been hearing, but it was still a shock, and to have to find out about it over the radio . . ."

Paul Riser: "We always felt that of course they'd take the nucleus of the company with them. I'm talking about the musicians, arrangers and engineers, the people who did the real work down in the trenches. But I never even got an offer. I think the truth was that they wanted to take as few people as possible who knew the history back here and how things were really created."

Uriel Jones: "For awhile, we were all looking forward to going to California with him, but they wouldn't give us no kind of guarantee. It was just tossed off, 'Oh, come on out. We'll still use you.' There was no talk of helping us relocate, and suddenly we were no longer going to be on salary. So a lot of us chose to just stay home. We didn't feel like we could do all that relocating ourselves on the basis of some vague promise." The only one of the Funk Brothers who remained under contract was James Jamerson, and this was only because Berry Gordy personally insisted that the increasingly erratic bassist not be fired.

But even Detroit-bred critic Dave Marsh, as passionate a fan of Motown's music as you're ever likely to find, sees an inevitability in this beyond Gordy's desire to be a movie mogul. "My guess is that it had as much to do with the '70s becoming the age of technologically-produced records," he states. "Technique really becomes a massive issue. This is heretical to say, but the Detroit studios were outmoded. The limitations of that studio – which for years had been Motown's greatest asset – suddenly come into play. The peculiarities of that room were once a huge advantage, but recording in the '70s was not about room sound, and there was really no way you could import the technology into that room.

"To the extent that popular music-making has anything organic about it, there's a relatively natural cycle in which any group of musicians can retain its currency. I would argue that if you take the Motown musicians from the earliest days of the Joe Hunter-led band of the late '50s through to this point – from Money to *What's Going On* – that's as long a run as any group has ever had. Certainly longer than the Muscle Shoals crew, a longer run than the Stax musicians. Collectively speaking, this group of people was past its peak, and there's no shame in that. They weren't past it as individual musicians, but in their collective ability to cut the contemporary dance records that the '70s would be about. Clearly they weren't past their creative peak, or *What's Going On* wouldn't exist."

The flesh-and-blood metaphor for this development is Stevie Wonder. The child genius who was taken under the wing of the Funk Brothers and was initiated into the mysteries of music by these masters grew up to be a mature artist who, thanks to the miracle of modern overdubbing technology, played nearly all the instruments on his records himself.

Chief engineer Mike McClain called one last gathering of the Audio Recording & Drinking Society for the sorrowful mission of dismantling Studio B and the mixing rooms. (Studio A was to be maintained for the occasional session that might be needed.) His brethren from all over the city heeded the call. Even 70-year-old Jimmy Syracuse, the owner of United Sound, where Berry had cut his first hits a lifetime ago, showed up to lend a hand. Gordy himself was there with his sleeves rolled up and a screwdriver in his hand, as he'd been when the family gathered to build Hitsville plank by plank in 1960. This last mission was accomplished over a couple of intense weekends. Guy Costa cherry-picked whatever he fancied for the studios out on the Coast. The rest was sold to other studios around Detroit, or junked. The assembly line ended here.

Barrett Strong: "I've always kept pretty much to myself. I never listened to gossip or hung out much, so I wasn't exactly tuned in to what was going on. It seemed like I woke up one day, went to the studio and found that the whole place had been abducted by aliens, like some big rocket ship had carried everybody away. Turned out it had – to Los Angeles."

"It was kind of strange," David Van De Pitte says of the period when the company was pulling up stakes. "People didn't know what was supposed to happen. Many of them thought that Berry was going to move the entire operation out there, lock stock and barrel. I think everybody here was holding their breath, waiting for the telephone call saying, 'OK, there's a plane ticket waiting for you at the airport, we'll find you a place to stay, you start work again on Monday.' It was terribly unrealistic, I guess. When I think back on it now, it was almost surreal; all these people in a daze waiting for the phone to ring."

Hardest hit, of course, were the lower-level functionaries. They all, no matter how lowly their functions, had been encouraged to think of themselves as members of Motown's extended family. When the company moved west they found out exactly how far the family extended. In the end the company's established stars lost nothing. The artists who really got hurt were those on the rungs below. Even though they weren't company priorities, as long as they were part of the Motown family they had the hope that one day they, like the Originals, might break through and have their moment in the spotlight. When Andrew Loog Oldham would come in to produce records for the ill-conceived Rare Earth label, he saw them everywhere. "The people they'd send to the airport to pick you up were wonderful drivers," he says, "but they all thought they were going be in the Temptations. They were just waiting their turn."

Steve Smith: "The employees felt hurt, but the city felt hurt even more. I saw it every day in the people I'd run into around town, in stores or bars or in the street.

Outside of the car industry, Motown was the one thing in Detroit that made everybody proud. You know, a sports team can have a great season and lift a whole city up, but Motown did it year in, year out. It was like winning the World Series every year."

For all that Motown meant to Detroit – financially, emotionally, and in a public relations sense – Berry Gordy had always had a lukewarm relationship with his hometown. He came out of a family that built whatever it had with its own hands, that had circled the familial wagons tightly in response to an environment that, though it was becoming predominantly African-American, was still controlled by a white power structure that had no interest in promoting black enterprise. All races and creeds could work together on the assembly line, play together on athletic teams, and make music together in the clubs and recording studios, but the seat of power was the same snowy complexion it had always been, and division was how it maintained control of its conquests.

Though its people responded immediately to Gordy's musical vision, the city had never really gotten it. "He mainly records blues, gospel and jazz numbers and is working into polkas," is how one early newspaper story assessed the Motown operation. When the label's success made it too large to ignore, the city's token acknowledgement dripped condescension. By the time Detroit got around to honoring Berry Gordy Jr as its "Small Businessman of the Year" in 1965, he was already presiding over an international empire, the world's largest independent record company, and America's biggest business of African-American ownership. Apart from The Big Three automakers (Ford, Chrysler, General Motors), nobody put more money into the city coffers than Berry Gordy. *Small Businessman of the Year?* It wasn't even funny as a joke.

No, there was not a lot of love lost between Berry Gordy and City Hall. He felt he was treated like a second-class citizen of Detroit, a prophet without honor in his own hometown. As a citizen of Los Angeles, he was treated like a king but could still dine anonymously in public, the golf courses were open 365 days a year and Vegas was but a short plane ride away. We can't say for sure because Mr Gordy does not grant interviews, but one can easily imagine that, when faced with choosing between the two, he simply thought, "Who needs this shit?" and junked his winter suits. In what sounded suspiciously like a parting slap, when Motown left town it was announced that the company's midwest promotion would henceforth be handled out of Chicago. When that announcement was made in June 1972, Detroit was waist-deep in plans for a Berry Gordy Day. The idea was unceremoniously flushed.

There are no facts and figures that can communicate what was lost with Motown's departure, because it was only partially about economics. The tone of Gordy's exit may have been set by his relations with the city power structure, but the impact of the move was felt deeply by every individual within a 100-mile radius of the Motor City – eventually in their pocketbooks, but immediately in their hearts and souls. To paraphrase the late Lester Bangs, never again would Detroiters agree about anything as they'd agreed about their civic pride in the music of Motown. Seen in this light, Inner City Blues takes on added shades of poignancy, and a haunted sort of prescience. It foreshadows Detroit's decline in the wake of Motown's abandonment, and the empty playground in which Marvin is standing on the back album cover becomes what was left behind.

The city has never really recovered from the departure of Motown, however inevitable that exit may have been for Berry Gordy. Automotive challenges from around the globe can sometimes still be beaten back (though Chrysler has had a more difficult time of late dealing with the buy-in "partnership" of the German automaker Daimler), and the city periodically proclaims a renaissance based on something or other, but there is an emptiness at the heart of this town that all its solutions thus far have failed to address. As this is being written, the Motor City is banking on casino gambling and new sports stadiums for its turnaround, two avenues that have never been shown to lead to an improvement in the quality of urban life around them. And, though Detroit is presently home to two musical trends of contemporary significance – techno and the dirty white boy rap of Eminem and Kid Rock – neither has the power nor the inclination to collect the city's shattered fragments and fashion from them something resembling a collective spirit. Thirty year later, Detroit still suffers from a broken heart.

(A former Motown executive recalls a Los Angeles dinner party in the late '70s attended by both Berry Gordy and Coleman A. Young, the latter having been elected Detroit's first black mayor the year after Gordy formally renounced his Motor City citizenship. By this account Young, one of the famed Tuskegee airmen and a target of everyone from the Red Squads of the '50s and '60s to the FBI, was pleading with Gordy to publicly re-establish a hometown presence. The mayor desperately wanted the positive PR this symbolic gesture would confer upon his struggle to establish Detroit as America's first African-

American metropolis. Mr Gordy gave him an immediate and final one-word response: "No.")

An all too literal stone's throw from the glittering casinos, and after a decade of unparalleled American prosperity, you can still find the blighted neighborhoods of Inner City Blues, seemingly untouched since the fiery uprising in the summer of 1967. From certain angles Detroit can resemble a bombed-out European city in the aftermath of World War II – the rubble of buildings left to nature for demolition, entire blocks flattened by conflagration or neglect, decaying gaps in the city checkerboard that look like Keith Richard's smile in the photos marked "before".

The city was not the only loser when Motown moved west. Though Gordy's forays into film, theater and television have produced mixed results at best – especially when one considers what was sacrificed – Motown continued to be a successful entity through the '70s and beyond. Any label that boasted Marvin Gaye, the Jackson 5, Stevie Wonder, Diana Ross, Rick James and Lionel Richie was bound to shift heavy units, but there was also no denying that, in its shiny offices on Sunset, Motown was now just another successful record company on the Boulevard. The first two Los Angeles projects, the Jackson

5 and Lady Sings The Blues, were spectacular successes. They were also heights the transplanted company would never scale again. Though Berry Gordy might see it differently, from the moment Motown departed Detroit, its bottom line would always be the strength of the catalog that was built in the city it left behind.

The executives moved, the artists moved, and even some of the Funk Brothers were persuaded to try their luck in the warm California sun for a time, but the spirit could not be transplanted. Berry Gordy had created a mighty empire, but he did not create the spirit that breathed life into it. He felt it, recognised it, encouraged and channeled it, but he could not copyright it or claim ownership of it or renegotiate the terms of its contract. He could march his streamlined army over the Rocky Mountains and down into Hollywood on elephants tattooed with the blue Motown logo, but this was the one thing he couldn't take with him.

Motown was the mightiest musical empire the world has ever seen. It will remain so, no matter how many (or how few) intergalactic corporate conglomerates wind up swallowing the whole entertainment business, because it was organic – rooted in a time and a place and a cast of characters that could only have existed there and then. It had nothing to do with strength on paper. We will never be that naïve and stupid as a culture again, and in some ways it was the *naïveté* and stupidity that allowed all these people to come together so selflessly to make this miraculous thing happen.

It has frequently been speculated that Detroit's secret might be in the water. Actually, it was in the work. For the better part of the 20th century the auto industry was a magnet for workers from all over the world. Detroit was a city of hard work and teamwork. Hard workers also play hard, which in a grossly simplified nutshell is why the Motor City became an entertainment center. With Detroit no longer booming, the dry-up of what had been a constant infusion of new blood is also the nutshell explanation for Detroit's decline as an entertainment center. The city is still considered one of the best *audiences* in the world, but is now only a sporadic producer of significant music.

Despite this, the people of Detroit, who have always been the city's greatest asset, find a way to survive and keep the flame burning. The machinery may have moved or been junked, but the human heartbeat will not be stilled. "I heard Robert Gordy say that the reason they left Detroit was that there was no more talent here," says Paul Riser, his voice rising in anger. "What a stupid, ignorant notion. I resent it to this day. Having to deal with that mentality in our administrators, it's a wonder we did anything worth remembering at all."

Hank Cosby: "Whenever anybody brings up the Motown Sound, I tell people the sound is still here in Detroit. The company left but the sound stayed. As soon as they started cutting records in LA it was obvious that it wasn't the same. We had the incredible system of musicians, arrangers and producers, sure, but it was more than that. It's what existed *between* these people, and what they were all connected *to*. That's the cord that got cut when the company left town.

"Detroit has always been a musical town. The kids in school were studying music like mad. Cass Technical High School was an amazing place. The mother of the great jazz baritone player Pepper Adams was a teacher there, and they had a Russian gentleman who was a monster talent. A lot of famous and influential names passed through Cass Tech. You learned so much music there that when you graduated you already had the equivalent of two years' college education. Now everywhere you look they seem to be cutting back on music education in the schools. Didn't the people who make these decisions learn *anything* from what we did?

"But you can't keep that spirit down. It's still here. What's happened is that it's gone back to the church; that's where you'll find it. You go to some of these churches around Detroit, oh man you can't hardly sit still with all the stuff these young people are playing. And the singing! You'll hear better singing in church than you'll find anywhere on the radio. Where else is soul music gonna go?"

Johnny Bristol: "In some ways Marvin Gaye represented the soul of Motown to me. In his heart he was a truly kind man, especially if you got to know him before the success caused other problems in his life. I remember when I was 19, we'd pool our money for a pack of cigarettes and a couple of Cokes just so we could sit around for a few hours more and try to figure out the secrets of music. This was before there was a Motown, over in the little place at St Antoine and Farnsworth streets where Anna Records was based. That was a Marvin Gaye very few people got to know. He was the first one to jump on the piano or drums whenever anyone expressed the slightest desire to play.

"Now, I love and totally respect Berry Gordy. I would give him everything I owned if he needed it, without question. But the public seems to have the picture of Mr Gordy waving his magic wand and this garden suddenly blooming. That's not the way it was. Everybody at the company had as much passion for the music, and the desire to succeed, as Mr Gordy did. For one thing, that was the standard he set, and you wouldn't last long if you didn't measure up. But Motown was built by every single person who ever worked there. Some of us don't get the recognition we deserve; other people will never even be *named*. But every one of us knows what we did, and so our pride doesn't really need public validation. We know."

But thanks to Berry Gordy – and sometimes, as with *What's Going On*, in spite of him – we have the works of art this collective spirit moved these mere mortals to create. Like all art, their recordings are only the preserved residue of those white-hot creative experiences, yet they conduct enough of its heat 30 years later that we are still warmed whenever we hear them. But those through whom that spirit moved directly have a more personal and complex relationship with their accomplishments.

"After a time I had to leave Detroit and move back to Mississippi, where my life has been a little bit better," says guitarist Eddie Willis, one of the shrinking order of Funk Brotherhood. "Every time I hear one of the records I helped make on the radio I still get a little pissed off. I talked about this all the time with Robert White before he passed on. You say 'I was on that record,' and people look at you like 'yea, sure,' like you're puttin' them on.

Happens to this day. Robert couldn't take that, and after a while he wouldn't even speak of it.

"I went back up to Detroit for Earl Van Dyke's funeral, and went to the Motown Museum just to look around. I walked down into the studio, and my knees were shaking, believe me. I had to leave out of there. It seemed like I started hearing all this noise. Wasn't no real noise – it was something only I could hear. It was like the ghost of all these voices rising up at the same time. I really heard that, as this noise that was only meant for me to hear. I had to leave my family down in there and go outside on West Grand Boulevard to get some air. I had to get away from the noise . . . all those voices . . ."

One wonders if Berry Gordy Jr hears those voices himself. "You grow, and you get over the indignities," says Richard Morris. "The things Berry could control he did his best with, and I have no problem with him now. To have been a part of the Motown history was the greatest experience of my life. But I'm here, I'm alive, and I'm still moving forward. Berry must have, what, $700 million or $800 million by now? The man feels he can't come out of his house without 17 bodyguards. He walks around surrounded by the LAPD. What kind of life can that be?"

Afterword: Come And Get These Memories

GEORGIA WARD WAS THE LAST OF THE Motowners, the longest-serving employee of, and last link to the little record company that started on West Grand Boulevard in Detroit. She had survived the Donovan Building, the move to Los Angeles, and the transfer of the company's assets to successive corporate stewards. As Director of Motown Archives, she maintained the logbooks and massive file card system of session and songwriter information that became the basic map by which musical archaeologists would begin their excavations of the glory that was Motown.

So how was Georgia Ward's 34 years of hard work rewarded? Did they throw her a going-away party with a cake frosted with the Motown logo? Did they present her with a gold watch, or perhaps a diamond album award to symbolise how much the blood and sweat of all the little people who built Motown had ultimately come to mean to their corporate bottom line?

No. In 2000, with Georgia Ward only a year from full retirement somebody deep in the bowels of the corporation that had absorbed Motown Records left a voicemail message informing Ms Ward that her position had been eliminated and her services were no longer required.

Epilogue: Los Angeles

When would the war stop? That's what I wanted to know ... the war inside my soul.

Marvin Gaye

APRIL 1, 1984. FOLLOWING A HEATED ARGUMENT that had turned into an ugly physical confrontation, 70-year-old Marvin Pentz Gay Sr walked into his son's bedroom carrying a .38 revolver and, from a distance of no more than six feet, shot Marvin Gaye through the heart. That would have been enough to kill him, but Gay Sr shuffled closer and put another bullet into the dying body of his eldest son. Had he lived, the singer would have celebrated his 45th birthday the next day.

What's Going On had transformed Marvin into the

Artist with a capital A that he'd always longed to be recognised as. He was not destined to be the black Sinatra or the next Nat King Cole as he'd once wished, but he was granted the opportunity to become something far greater: the real Marvin Gaye. He would never surpass the heights he achieved here, but in a sense he didn't try. *What's Going On* was as liberating to Marvin as it was to any other Motown artist, and that included the freedom not to follow this path. Instead, he used this freedom to let the many Marvins within him off the leash. He explored sensuality and sexuality in records like Let's Get It On and I Want You with the same intensity with which he'd worshipped on *What's Going On*. In *Here My Dear* he nakedly assessed the rubble of his marriage to Anna and, with *In Our Lifetime*, an album Motown released before Gaye had completed it, he lays bare the torment of his deeply divided self.

The succeeding years saw him become the Superstar (with a capital S) his ego had also demanded. Yet the fruits of his success as a Superstar ultimately tasted no less bitter than his early Motown hits, exacerbating the depression and exaggerating the conflicts that haunted his every accomplishment. After wandering through the deserts of Hawaii and Europe (proof that a man can see any landscape as barren), he returned in 1982 with the brilliant Sexual Healing. The song confirmed his melodic sensual mastery, while the use of the word "healing" harked back to the spiritual balm of *What's Going On*. It won him the Grammy that he'd always felt (rightly) that he'd been unjustly denied for that earlier work. There was every reason to think that Marvin Gaye was looking at a bright tomorrow.

Sadly, that assumption was wrong. Dead wrong. With his professional rebound all the demons came rushing back in as well, and he was in no shape to offer much resistance. By that awful April Fool's Day of '84, he had retreated to a room in the house he'd bought for his parents in the Crenshaw district of Los Angeles. There, in a darkened room he seldom left, he sank ever deeper into a chemically-fueled depression. This eventually degenerated into a full-blown cocaine psychosis that caused even his beloved mother to characterise what he'd become as "a monster".

Down the hall his father, the failed preacher who'd once thundered against the evils of drink, was now brooding darkly through a daily bottle of vodka. "I celebrate Marvin's genius," Gay Sr had told David Ritz. "I honor my son's talents and bask in his reflected glory." According to most, however, Father Gay withheld acknowledgement of his son's accomplishments and, rather than basking in that reflected glory, the more appropriate verb would be "seethed". Not only had he failed to beat the rebellious spirit out of the boy, but he had been made to watch that spirit carry the son soaring far beyond the father.

"He could never accept that his son had become this larger-than-life figure when he'd never gotten beyond the storefronts as a preacher," Joe Schaffner believes. "Marvin had this totally love/hate situation with his father, but from the father's end there wasn't any love that I ever saw. He was *totally* jealous of the success his son had achieved. One time Marvin had been paid in cash and he laid it on the bed, telling his father that he could have any or all of it. It was more money than Mr Gay had seen in his life, and it made him hate his son even more. Marvin bought him a big Fleetwood Cadillac. Every year there'd be a new car so that he could ride around town and pretend he was this ultra-successful preacher. As long as his son wasn't there. But the minute Marvin shows up, then people might get the idea the car was bought *for* him. For years he had been taken care of by Marvin. He was being reminded of it continually. Mentally I think it ate away at him."

Two human bombs were ticking. The explosion had been decades in the making, and Schaffner is among those who see a fitting symmetry in the way it played out. "I look at it as a destined situation," he says. "God saw it right that he be killed by his father, rather than over-dosing or doing himself in. But to have his father, who'd inflicted such violence on the child, inflict the final violence on his son gave a kind of closure. His father hated him so much that he finally got up the courage to do what he'd wanted to do a long time before." Though it manifested in many ways, both of their lives had come to be defined by the struggle between them, so perhaps there was a tragic appropriateness to the final resolution coming face-to-face.

Still others have read into Marvin's actions that fateful day a provocation tantamount to suicide. The pummeling he administered to his father may have been payback for a lifetime of abuse, first physical and then mental. But it was Marvin who had recently provided Gay Sr with a handgun, knowing full well that his father had long and loudly proclaimed that he'd kill Marvin if he ever raised a finger against him. In the end, the greatest tragedy was not the manner in which Marvin Gaye was taken, but that he was taken unnecessarily. Help in dealing with his demons was as easily available to him as the powders with which he chose to medicate himself, but his ego – the very same ego that drove his artistic accomplishments – prevented him from asking for it, or accepting it when, despite his obstinacy, it was offered to him.

Of course, Marvin had already provided all of us with medication from a higher source when he recorded *What's Going On*. This is an album that will be listened to for as long as there is music. Some records the future will listen to and marvel at how richly they captured their moment in time. This is what they will hear first in Marvin's masterpiece, but then, like so many before them, they will hear more, and more again. They will hear the most a man – and music – can be.

But the museums and history books are crowded with artists who couldn't live up to their art, and the sadness of the album comes with the retrospective knowledge that it was ultimately of less help to its creator than to any of its listeners. If the divinely inspired *What's Going On* couldn't save Marvin Gaye, I know that the profound social concern and warm spiritual embrace of this music has been beneficial to countless souls over the years. "Marvin is as much a minister as any man in the pulpit," the Reverend Jesse Jackson told Time magazine in its 1971 story devoted to *What's Going On*. Ultimately the word "minister" is more properly used here as a verb – to minister, to give aid and comfort. It offers these priceless things at the cost of an ordinary compact disc, and it provides them every time you hit "play".

I know this from personal experience. Like Marvin, I have fought a lifelong battle with intense and debilitating depression. Unlike him, I have benefited greatly from modern medicine as practiced by a few good men and women. But, along with family and friends, this album has also been a lifelong companion, and has helped greatly on those occasions when the pit seemed bottomless. The most recent onslaught came as I struggled to complete this book, a task that only weeks ago seemed utterly hopeless. Of the considerable help I received, I can testify that the strength and compassion of *What's Going On* were instrumental in my rescue and recovery. It is a work that reawakens you to the pain that exists in the world outside the one the sufferer has constructed for himself, and this is the first step toward building a bridge back. Then it provides you with the tools to get the job of healing done. This album has never failed me, and I know it will be there when I need it again.

In this I know I am not alone. Many thousands of people have experienced their own variation of this; for a record that aimed at the universal and hit the bullseye, each individual's experience of *What's Going On* is remarkably personal. And the final measure of the album's worth is that it continues to work its wonders on more people every day, many of them young men and women who were not even born when Marvin first transmitted his message.

"I was approached once by a guy I didn't know, who said he had a story he *had* to tell me," Frankie Gay whispered slowly. Marvin's younger brother was recovered from a recent cranial operation when we spoke, but still tended to lean on each word for support as he went. "He said that one time he was intent upon hurting somebody, hurting them *bad*. But as he was on his way out the door to commit this violence, he heard Marvin singing What's Going On over the radio and it stopped him in his tracks. Something in that song touched him, and he didn't go. He understood that he had choices. My first thought was, 'Wow, man, if Marvin only knew . . .'. I'd always been proud of my brother, but this made me overflow with pride. He was trying to find a way to talk about issues between people in a way that brought them love. He did it, man. He did it, and it changed the world."

Amen.

Timeline

FEBRUARY 3, 1967 Producer Norman Whitfield begins work on
I Heard It Through The Grapevine for Marvin Gaye.
Motown will reject the single as "too different".

APRIL 20, 1967 Ain't No Mountain High Enough by Marvin
Gaye and Tammi Terrell released.

APRIL 30, 1967 The hippie community's "Love-In Detroit" at the
city park on Belle Isle turns into a police riot.

JULY 23, 1967 What will be described as "the worst race riot in
American history" and leave 43 dead is sparked when
Detroit police raid an after-hours club in the black neigh-
borhood at 12th and Clairmount.

SEPTEMBER 28, 1967 The Gladys Knight And The Pips version of
I Heard It Through The Grapevine released.

OCTOBER 14, 1967 Tammi Terrell collapses on-stage at a show
with Marvin Gaye at Hampton Sydney College in Virginia.

APRIL 4, 1968 Dr Martin Luther King Jr assassinated in

Memphis.

JUNE 5, 1968 Senator Robert F. Kennedy shot in Los Angeles; dies the following day.

JUNE 7, 1968 Bobby Taylor records his lead vocal on the Richard Morris/Marvin Gaye production of The Bells, which is rejected by Motown.

JUNE 23, 1968 Though not officially recognised by the US Government as a war, the "conflict" in Vietnam becomes the longest war in American history.

AUGUST 1968 Marvin Gaye LP *In The Groove* released, containing the album track I Heard It Through The Grapevine.

AUGUST 21, 1968 Bobby Taylor records a new set of lyrics for The Bells. This version is also rejected.

AUGUST 26, 1968 Democratic National Convention opens in Chicago. Television cameras capture hundreds of anti-war protesters and ordinary citizens being beaten bloody by police, leading to the chant "The whole world is watching."

SEPTEMBER 24, 1968 Keep On Lovin' Me Honey by Marvin Gaye and Tammi Terrell released. It was the last of the duo's hits to actually feature Terrell. The following three featured the stand-in vocals of Valerie Simpson.

NOVEMBER 30, 1968 Grapevine released as a single after Chicago airplay as an album track lights up the phones. *In The Groove* is quickly reissued as *I Heard It Through The Grapevine*.

DECEMBER 4, 1968 The Originals record their lead vocals on the track for The Bells. The lyric has been rewritten a third time, and is now called Baby I'm For Real. Motown rejects this record as well.

MAY 15, 1969 The violent "People's Park" confrontation between protesters and police in Berkeley, CA prompts Obie Benson to begin sketching the song What's Going On.

JULY 1969 Originals LP *Green Grow The Lilacs* released, containing the album track Baby I'm For Real.

JULY 20, 1969 Apollo 11 lands on the moon.

AUGUST, 12, 1969 Baby I'm For Real released as a single after Detroit airplay as an album track lights up the phones. *Green Grow The Lilacs* is quickly reissued as *Baby I'm For Real*.

OCTOBER 15, 1969 Vietnam Moratorium Day is observed by millions.

JANUARY 9, 1970 The Bells by the Originals, which retains only a few words from the Bobby Taylor And The Vancouvers versions, is released.

MARCH 16, 1970 Tammi Terrell dies at Graduate Hospital in Philadelphia.

MARCH 20, 1970 Marvin speaks at Tammi Terrell's funeral in Philadelphia.

MAY 4, 1970 National Guardsmen kill four students during protests at Kent State University in Ohio.

JUNE 1, 1970 Marvin cuts the basic track for What's Going On at Hitsville (Motown Studio A). On the same session he also cuts an early version of Just To Keep You Satisfied for the Originals, which he will later appropriate (keeping some of the Originals' backing vocals) for *Let's Get It On*.

JULY 6, 7 AND 9, 1970 Lead vocals, backing vocals and instrumental overdubs on What's Going On at Studio B.

JULY 10, 1970 Additional overdubs on What's Going On at Studio A.

SEPTEMBER 21, 1970 Strings added to What's Going On at Golden World (Motown Studio B).

SEPTEMBER 1970 Marvin Gaye compilation album *Super Hits* released.

JANUARY 21, 1971 The What's Going On single finally released. Its B-side is an earlier, slower take on God Is Love.

MARCH 17, 1971 Basic tracks for the rest of side one of *What's Going On* – What's Happening Brother, Flyin' High (In The Friendly Sky), Save The Children, God Is Love and an unused take of Mercy Mercy Me (The Ecology) – recorded at Studio A.

MARCH 19, 1971 Basic track for Mercy Mercy Me recut, along with tracks for side two of *What's Going On* – Right On, Wholy Holy and Inner City Blues (Make Me Wanna Holler) – recorded at Studio B.

MARCH 24, 1971 Strings and horns on Wholy Holy recorded at Studio B.

MARCH 26, 1971 Strings and horns added to side one of *What's Going On* and Inner City Blues at Studio B.

MARCH 27–30, 1971 Lead vocals, background vocals, and miscellaneous instrumental overdubs added to all tracks at Studio B.

APRIL 5, 1971 Album mixed by Steve Smith with Marvin Gaye at The Motown Center (Woodward Avenue).

MAY 5, 1971 Having decided the album is not finished after all, Marvin adds new and additional vocals to Mercy Mercy Me, Right On, Wholy Holy and Inner City Blues at the Sound Factory in Los Angeles.

MAY 6, 1971 Album remixed by Lawrence Miles with Marvin

Gaye at the Motown Studio ("Hitsville West") in Los Angeles.

MAY 21, 1971 *What's Going On* released.

JULY 1971 Mercy Mercy Me (The Ecology) b/w Sad Tomorrows released.

OCTOBER 1971 Mono remix of Inner City Blues (Make Me Wanna Holler) b/w Wholy Holy released.

MAY 1, 1972 "Marvin Gaye Day" in Washington DC. His concert that evening at the Kennedy Center Auditorium would be the only time he performed the complete *What's Going On* live.

MARCH 2001 To commemmorate the 30th anniversary of *What's Going On*, Universal Music releases a 2-CD deluxe edition of the album. It includes the original Detroit mix, the Marvin Gaye Day concert, and miscellaneous treats that include an early version of Distant Lover.

Studio information supplied by Harry Weinger.

Bibliography

BOOKS

Christgau, Robert *Rock Albums Of The '70s* (Da Capo Press, New York 1981)

Davis, Sharon *Marvin Gaye* (Proteus Books, London/New York 1984)

George, Nelson *Where Did Our Love Go* (St Martin's Press, New York 1985)

Gordy, Berry *To Be Loved* (Headline Books, London 1994; Warner Books, New York 1994)

Hirshey, Gerri *Nowhere To Run: The Story Of Soul Music* (Macmillan, London 1984; Times Books, New York 1984)

Marsh, Dave *The Heart Of Rock & Soul* (New American Library, New York 1989)

Reeves, Martha *Dancing In The Street* (Hyperion, New York 1994)

Ritz, David *Divided Soul* (Michael Joseph, London 1985; McGraw Hill, New York 1985)

Ryan, Jack *Recollections: The Detroit Years* (Whitlaker Marketing, Whitmore Lake MI 1982)

Singleton, Raynoma *Gordy Berry, Me and Motown* (Contemporary Books, Chicago 1990)

Slutsky, Allan (aka Dr Licks) *Standing In The Shadows of Motown: The Life and Music of James Jamerson* (Dr Licks Publishing, Wynnewood, PA 1989)

Smith, Suzanne E. *Dancing In The Street: Motown And The Cultural Politics Of Detroit* (Harvard University Press, London / Cambridge, MA 1999)

Turner, Steve *Trouble Man* (Michael Joseph, London 1998; Ecco Press, New York 2000)

Waller, Don *The Motown Story* (Charles Scribner's Sons, New York 1985)

Whitall, Susan *Women Of Motown* (Avon Books, New York 1998)

Wilson, Mary *Dreamgirl & Supreme Faith* (UK pub info unknown; Cooper Square Press, New York 1999)

PERIODICALS

"Berry Gordy Jr – Detroit's Record King" Ken Barnard (Detroit Free Press December 26, 1962)

"Million Dollar Music In Four Flats" Earl B. Dowdy (Detroit News July 25, 1965)

"Motown's Going Uptown In Boss' Palatial New Digs" Elspeth Beier (Detroit Free Press March 2, 1967)

"Motown Engine Still Runs, But 2 Big Groups Misfire" Lee Winfrey (Detroit Free Press October 1968)

"The Story Behind The Sour Notes At Motown" Tom Ricke

(Detroit Free Press November 22, 1968)

"Lions Turn Down A Melodic Touch" Jack Saylor (Detroit
News July 29, 1970)

"A Visit With Marvin Gaye" Ben Fong-Torres (Rolling Stone
April 27, 1972)

"Motown's Singing, Sparring Star" Tom Zito (Washington Post
April 30, 1972)

"Motown Exiting City A Little At A Time" Chuck Thurston
(Detroit Free Press June 9, 1972)

"What's Behind Motown Move" Bill Gray (Detroit News June
25, 1972)

"The Spirit, The Flesh And Marvin Gaye" Tim Cahill (Rolling
Stone April 11, 1974)

"Trouble Man" Michael Goldberg (Rolling Stone May 10, 1984)

"A Voice Set Free" David Ritz (Rolling Stone May 10, 1984)

"The Genius And The Tragedy Of Marvin Gaye" Bob Talbert
(Detroit Free Press November 25, 1990)

"Like Getting A High Five From God" Neely Tucker (Detroit
Free Press September 15, 1991)

"Master Of The Motown Sound" D.W. Fostle (Audio November
1997)

When, in December 1968, BEN EDMONDS met the MC5 in the back room of the legendary New York art bar, Max's Kansas City, they advised the impressionable young New Englander to move to Detroit. This he did, becoming an editor on the fabled *Creem* magazine and he hasn't looked back since. His writing has subsequently appeared in *Rolling Stone*, *NME* and the *Los Angeles Times* and he's also been in artist management (The Doors), production (Iggy Pop's *Kill City*) and all manner of record company work. Ben is currently MOJO magazine's man in America.